THE LAST NOSTALGIA

DATE DUE

Demco, Inc. 38-293

THE LAST NOSTALGIA

Poems 1982–1990

BY JOE BOLTON

Edited by Donald Justice

THE UNIVERSITY OF ARKANSAS PRESS

03 02 01 00   5 4 3 2

Photographs of Joe Bolton courtesy of Tonya Parsons
Designer: Chiquita Babb/Septima Designs

Library of Congress Cataloging-in-Publication Data
Bolton, Joe, 1961–
      The last nostalgia : poems, 1982–1990 / by Joe Bolton ; edited by
      Donald Justice.
            p. cm.
      ISBN 1-55728-558-6 (pbk. : alk. paper)
      I. Justice, Donald Rodney, 1925–   . II. Title.
      PS3552.O58775L37   1999
      811'.54—dc21   99-10535
                                                                              CIP

Acknowledgments

The contents of the following previously published books are included in *The Last Nostalgia*:

Breckinridge County Suite, copyright 1987, 1989 Joe Bolton; published by The Cummington Press, Omaha, Nebraska.

Days of Summer Gone, copyright 1990 Joe Bolton; published by The Galileo Press, Baltimore, Maryland.

The editor wishes to thank the following magazines, where many of the poems in the other sections of *The Last Nostalgia* first appeared:

Agni: "Aubade"
The Antioch Review: "Diptych"
Apalachee Quarterly: "South Boulevard"
Arete: Forum for Thought: "Aphrodite Holding a Seashell"; "Ballroom Dancing in the Barrio"; "The Mississippi at Barfield, Arkansas"
Black Warrior Review: "Meditation at Kentucky Dam" (under title: "Towards Twenty-Four")
Blue Buildings: "Another Rainy Night"
Crazy Horse: "Adult Situations"; "The Circumstances"; "Cleaved Spheres"; "Death in Orange County"; "Rack!"; "Style"
Cumberland Poetry Review: "August Elegy"; "The Parthenon at Nashville"
Denver Quarterly: "Fin de Siécle"; "Near"
The Formalist: "Florida Twilight, 1905"; "Summer"; "To a Woman Passing By"; "The Years"; "Tropical Courtyard"
High Plains Literary Review: "Sardis Reservoir, Mississippi"
Indiana Review: "Hurricane"; "Little Testament"
Mid-American Review: "Tropical Lament"
The Nebraska Review: "In Memory of the Boys of Dexter, Kentucky"
The New Criterion: "Elegy at Summer's End"; "Hell and Back"; "Page"; "Soon"
The New Republic: "Childhood"
The North American Review: "Sherwood Anderson, 1912"
Northcoast View Monthly Magazine: "Laguna Beach Breakdown"; "The Lights at Newport Beach"
The Oxford American: "Lines for Hank Williams"; "Twilight" ; "Woodshedding: Kentucky, 1980" ; "Dawn: Washington, D.C. January 1, 1990"

Poetry: "Elegy for Roland Barthes"

Quarterly West: "The Beginning of Summer"; "Wild Horses"

Salamander: "A Couple of Suicide Cases"; "Ode to the Backs of a Woman's Knees"; "Stanzas on the Anniversary of Hart Crane's Death"; "The Woman with the Dog"

South Florida Poetry Review: "Tropical Deco"

Southern Poetry Review: "In Spring"

Tampa Review: "In Pieces"; "Tropical Watercolor: Sarasota"

Tampa Tribune: "Miami"

The Threepenny Review: "Daisy Miller in the Colosseum"; "Flamingos"

Wind: "Once in Autumn"

The Yale Review: "Tall Palms"

The editor is deeply grateful for the help of the following friends of the poet, without whose encouragement, research, and suggestions this book could not have been put together:

Jon Anderson, Rebecca Byrkit, Michael W. Cox, Robert Houston, William Logan, Steven Orlen, Tonya Parsons, Frank Steele, and of course Ed Bolton, the poet's father.

Contents

THE NEW CITIES OF THE TROPICS

ADULT SITUATIONS

Introduction

Joseph Edward Bolton was born on December 3, 1961, in Cadiz, Kentucky, and grew up in the western part of that state known as the Jackson Purchase. His parents were Ed Bolton and Nancy Foster, both from rural and small-town backgrounds, both schoolteachers. The young Bolton went off on a scholarship to the University of Mississippi for his freshman year but soon returned to Kentucky, where he took his B.A. at Western Kentucky University in Bowling Green. Thereafter, like other young writers of the time, he moved from one college writing program to another—Houston, Florida, Arizona—teaching as a graduate assistant and postponing his entry into "the real world." In the spring of 1990, as he neared the completion of his work for a degree at Arizona, it must have been disappointing that he had no good prospect of a job, but he could look forward to the book he had coming out later that year. Toward the end of March he turned in his master's thesis, a collection of poems he called *The Last Nostalgia*. The following day, March 30, in the early morning hours, he took his own life. There was no note.

It was as though the poet felt that his life's work was done. To a friend he had spoken of writing no more poems; he thought, half-seriously at least, of turning to murder mysteries. In any case, he was one who believed that a poet's best work was to be accomplished early, that the rest was anticlimax and decline. In this his high romantic spirit declared itself. The poet Jon Anderson, a good friend, spoke of Bolton's fascination with the "romance" of suicide, and there is no denying that this was a subject to which in his poems he could not resist coming back and back to. But it was only a part, albeit a deeply personal part, of his subject matter. It was the larger culture of his time that drew him and for which he apparently saw himself not as a spokesman so much as a representative or recorder. At first he turned, naturally enough, to his native South, and of that region he proved himself an observer at once sardonic and lovingly committed. Later, more expansively, it was America itself that became his subject, high culture and low. And in everything he took pleasure and found beauty. There is nothing, he wrote, "That is not beautiful or that will last."

A number of his poems deal with that side of the South which a generation of Southern storytellers has virtually made iconographic—the lower-middle-class life of rental apartments and loud neighbors, of motel rooms, of bars and highways, small towns and rundown urban neighborhoods. But

Bolton's style of looking and noticing is not the same as that of the story-tellers. He had a kind of helpless love for the subjects of his poems; and that, I think, cannot fairly be said of the writers whose fiction shares the locales of these poems. The tone that results is bracingly different.

Bolton was clearly place-sensitive. His poems had for him, as he some-times said, a strong sense of place, even when the place did not show up in the poem. But often it did show up, not only present but named, specified, as if the name of the place conferred a kind of actuality and authenticity. His moves from one part of the South to another can be charted from the poems—Mississippi, Texas, Florida, and, finally, out of the South to Arizona. But always he kept coming back to the Western Kentucky of his childhood, the home for him of memory.

Many of his poems have something of the character of journal or diary entries. Casual-seeming and rather unassuming reports of what is happen-ing or did once happen, they have an instant and easily won believability, far beyond that of most poetry. Not that they are what could be called confes-sional exactly: confession just does not seem the point of these poems. Effortlessly they transcend the merely anecdotal; they are always edging toward something emblematic. And they can be immensely moving in their modesty.

The early death of a writer tempts us to imagine what unfulfilled promise the future would have seen realized. We perhaps discover signs, real or illu-sory, of the maturing of some early brilliance. But in this poet's work I would find it hard to make a case for this kind of progress. The charm of the poems—and ultimately their worth—depends on a certain blazing youth-ful freshness allied with the doomed romantic spirit which haunts and drives them. The work may change over time but it does not change very much. Of his own poems Bolton said, "The scene is twilit, the mood existential, the outlook tragic." And this did not change, except perhaps to darken and grow weary. But there is all along a tangle of wonder and despair, a tangle which strikes me as indeed a mark of youth, but not rare either and certainly very sympathetic. Bolton in the end came to embody and give voice to a certain mixed attitude toward life—his attitude was, amidst all the deep despairs and despondencies, still the most intensely responsive, the most keenly appre-ciative imaginable.

Donald Justice
August, 1998

BRECKINRIDGE COUNTY SUITE

To a Young Kentucky Woman

Lord, it is time. The huge summer has gone by.
—Rainer Maria Rilke

There is no such thing as innocence in autumn,
Yet, it may be, innocence is never lost.
—Wallace Stevens

Did she feel that now, having met her father at last,
she was now truly bereaved and alone? That only when
you are truly alone can you begin to live? That when you truly
begin to live you must construct your own world and therefore
have no need for words written on paper, words that can only
give the shadow of a world already lived?
—Robert Penn Warren

I. The Ohio

Seven miles south of anywhere
You'd rather be, it is autumn.
What sweetened shrivels,
What shriveled falls,
And what fell is leaf-rot,
A sick rich scent on the air.

You are paling, you are bored,
You are zipping up your jacket
And walking into a dynamo
Of twilight and raw wind,
Tossing your hair as a brief bruise
Of pink scores the horizon.

Seven miles north, below the lights
From the bars and dance halls
Of small towns, the Ohio swells
With a cargo of barges,
And catfish twist through the bones
Of what never bothered to rise.

II. The Summer Loves

How deftly they undressed you,
Laid you down,
Their rough hands opening you like a flower
In a field of flowers, their faces
Dark with your dark.

—Boys, you'd say now, though you
Never minded much,

And once you'd got them out of their daddy's truck
And one good shirt, found them generally
Adequate for your purposes.

Hardly anything was ever said
At the time,
And little was ever said later that found its way
Back to you. Still, there must have been
Talk, for there is always talk.

They took their time, and when they
Came, you came.
And it was as if your own body betrayed you then—
As if only their body above yours kept you
From falling into the blue of sky.

III. The Prototypical Ghosts

The west field, wasted, seems day by day to recede
From the warped kitchen window where you stand in steam,
Your hand gone limp as the rag that won't drop from it.
Like worn-out records, your frail parents, aging

Even when you were born, in their dotage
Seem more and more the prototypical ghosts
Of themselves, as if fifty years of food
From the same gray land had turned them gray as the land.

They hardly make a sound now, unless it is
To rasp a vague complaint, half remember a year
That has forgotten them, or tap against the table
Some object that's outlasted its significance.

The old and the new songs of heartbreak sound the same.
It's only when the needle grinds in the grooves
That a sadness greater than your own comes on,
And the dead begin to live again, in you.

IV. Hard Country

It is, even now, a hard country to live in.

Full summer is invisible fire under cypresses
Dying of thirst,
And you think of the dog days it got too hot
To do much else but sit and sweat
And watch the ground bake till it cracked.

Or, wintering, it could be the New World:
The empty duskward distances
And killing promise of snow.
You still remember the night it fell to fifteen below.
You were sitting at the kitchen table,
Ten years old,
A blanket on your lap and a bowl
Of snow cream in front of you.
Your mother was stoking the stove.
You saw, through the window, the west field
Silvered with snow and starlight. Saw
The figure of your father crossing the field,
And the load he carried curled in his arms:
A calf that had picked a bad night for being born.
He brought it in to warm by the stove,
Red ice of afterbirth melting into pools
And the poor thing's ears already frozen off.

Now, in autumn, walking the long mile
Back from the empty mailbox,
You can see the place, what's left of it:
Two Plymouths and a '34 Ford
Squat rusting, wheelless, home
To broken tools and rotten clothes, mice.
Gray barns and outbuildings lean graying.
And the white house is white
Only in memory,
For the photographs, too, have faded.
Back of the smokehouse, from limp fur, the skull
Of an eaten raccoon grins skyward.
You wonder if there was ever any glory to be had here,
And if not, then why, for two hundred years,
Anybody has bothered. . . .

A hard country to live in, yes,
But not a hard country in which to find
A place to drown oneself.
You think of water, of the names
Of water: Sinking River, Rough River Lake,
South Fork of the Panther.
And all of it flowing Ohioward, Gulfward.

For water everywhere rages to be with other water;
Or, held isolate in ponds, in the hoofprint
Of the thousand-pound heifer after rain,
Reflects the utter emptiness of sky.

And water is as empty as sky, only
Easier to fall into,
Heavier to breathe.

V. On the Square

It could be any Southern town you care to name:
Bank, diner, hardware store, lone traffic light.
Saturdays, you come to buy everything
That can't be grown, contrived, or done without.
Old men sit spitting on the courthouse steps.
A boy in a Camaro squeals, once, his wide new tires.
Women test their reflections in the windows of the shops
They pass, hoping to find some lost beauty restored.

And when those eyes, for a moment, hold yours, they seem
To hold some insolence. You think they think you
Are guilty of some crime beyond the crime
All are guilty of. And oh, my dear, they do!
                                    And so do you.

VI. The Sinking River at Stevensport

Closing your eyes, you can see
What nobody ever saw:
It is midnight, past midnight,
The figure just visible
In the moonless, dew-laden dark
Where river empties into
River, and the water makes
No sound, or a sound like time,
Which stands still now on the bank.
He, too, stands still on the bank,
Late-summer night wind whipping
The white linen of his coat—
For, yes, he always did have
A sense of style in such things.

Behind him, the white car shines
Under what starlight there is.
He stares at what stars there are
And remembers—or does he?—
The flowered dress he bought you
And raised above your waist here
So you could straddle his lap.
Does he think of the river
Lit at Louisville, where some-
Thing he can hardly admit
To himself happened?—happened
To you, though you both agreed
It was the best thing to do. . . .
Does he speak aloud now to
No one? Does he say a name?
Does he say your name before
He walks into the river?
Or does he just walk away?
You must believe both stories
Till the world makes up its mind.
Either way, the white car shines
As dawn lights the water, and
—All this behind your closed eyes—
That wide water seems to hold
The dead in their element.

VII. Making Love in a Colored Graveyard

Walking past the garden, you see it's grayed,
Okra withered to seed and sunflower
Self-decapitated. It is the hour
When you can hear the grass die, blade by blade.
Where are you going, hearing the grass die,
Casting no shadow under the sunless sky?

Daddy, take me to the colored graveyard!
It was spring, and you, a child, rode piggyback
On his shoulders past the newly-turned black
Fields soon to swell green, imagining you heard
Monsters from the woods taunting with shrill song
The bovine beasts who'd fatten all summer long.

He let you down at the edge of the woodslot
Where beech, black gum and pin oak formed a nave
Of incessant half-darkness, and a grave
Might lie unfound forever, save by fox or muskrat.
But knowing the place and its story, he showed you seven
Blank wafers of stone under that half-lit heaven.

And making you stand still and quiet, said:
"Sometimes, if you listen hard, you can hear—
And especially if you come in the fall of the year—
Them singing. It's the songs they sang for their dead."
But you, for all your listening, heard only
The creek running nearby, and thought the dead lonely.

Years later, in summer, you took your lover there;
And though the stones had sunk some, you found them
Among green fern and ginseng. Limb by limb,
The light climbed down through that tangle of leafy air.
You told him the story, then listened together, then laughed
When he pressed you against a moss-soft sassafras

And stopped your cry of *No, we can't, not here*
With his mouth over yours and his deft hands
Already undoing you. It was as if the land
Knew when you came together—when, in your ears,
Above bird-cry and leaf-stir, your blood rang.
And then, if only that once, the dead sang.

Now, coming back to the place in autumn,
You watch rose- and wine-colored leaves swirl down,
And, seeing the stones now barely break the ground,

Think: *So this is what it does to things, time.*
The creek leaf-choked, you can hear the grass die.
Under the clouds, come. Sit. Hear the grass die.

VIII. The Story

After the life is lived
And the world is what it is,
There is only the story:

At Stevensport, the Sinking River
Empties into the Ohio,
And the Ohio widens.

Or does the story perhaps precede
The living of it, as the new day
Seems to depend on the cock's cry?

And do the dead and the unborn occupy
The same dimensionless dimension,
Or are they simply where they seem to be?

It would be easy enough to say
What happened, could you only
Bring yourself to:
                            A girl—
No, a young woman—who has lived her life
With old-time parents on a farm
On what the Indians once called the Dark
And Bloody Ground, and who
Has a perhaps somewhat imprudent appetite
For things sensual, falls in love.
His speech and dress and manner
Are slightly strange to her at first, but she

Is taken with the simultaneous
Inward frailty and successful outward gesture
With which he lives in the world, of which
He seems already to have seen much.

In the summer of your first and one great love,
Stars flared nightly in the architecture of sky,
And the world opened up beneath that sky.
The scenes flash and fade now like summer starfall:
Parked in his white car down some dark road;
Driving to Owensboro and Bowling Green; dancing
In a little dive in Tell City, Indiana . . .
You see yourself—that self—like the portraits
Of those who, no longer living, live
In the flash and fade of a moment torn from time.

                    *

Once, the city lured her.
Once, watching the lights
Of Louisville come slowly on in summer dusk,
She thought . . . what?
That this would last forever?—or even
Outlast forever?
                    Later,
Going there to undo
What the two of you had done,
You saw how dirty-gray the city was,
As morning began and the poorer people rose
To the day's indecencies,
And you saw you were suddenly one of them. . . .
When it was over, you had to have him
Stop the car so you could throw up,
Then hugged yourself all the way home.

And she never caught sight of him again.

And so are left to remember the summer nights
When, half-drunk in your daddy's truck or his white car,

You'd take the hills and turns on Rough River Road
At seventy, just to feel your insides rise.
And laugh for surviving it, and look for shooting stars.

The white car was all that was left of him.
No body, or note, was ever discovered.
—Only the white car, shining in September dawn,
Beside the Sinking River at Stevensport. . . .
And which circumstances have, of course,
Led to speculation:
                    that he got you
Into trouble and couldn't stand himself for it;
That you, never good, drove him to it;
That he only wanted to make it look
As if he were dead, and is living it up
In Chicago or Indianapolis or some such place.

The rumors, unverified, multiply,
While the people you grew up with
Marry, buy farms, go bankrupt, get divorced,
And move off to the city, looking for work.

The night is starless, utterly still.

You are careful not to let these pieces
Of a narrative cohere
Into anything that might explain too much.

For you, who live in the world,
Must let the world
Remain ambiguous.

And it just wouldn't be right
To blame a drowned boy
For not floating up bloated,

Or not leaving a note,
Or perhaps not even
Drowning himself at all.

IX. The Storm

The big clock ticks off afternoon,
Time's brass teardrop hung
In dark cherrywood.

The radio, between three-minute tragedies
Heart-felt and with fiddles,
                 says storm,
And you turn it down
And pick up the phone just to see if it's gone dead,
Which it has,
           and the big clock ticks . . .

Until you are afraid.
—Not of the old house darkening
As the sky fills with fast clouds,
Or of your parents' deaths,
Or of dying,
Or of anything you could put your finger on
Or name.
           Shut the windows.
Call the cat inside, who's black
With gold-green eyes that know
                something's up.
Now wait.
Rub your raw hands, and wait. . . .
                  It hits.
Lightning makes terrible tattoos,
Slow *boom* of air exploding,
Then a faint crackling,
And the whole process repeating itself
Till rain falling sheet on heavy sheet
Drowns out sound and remembrance
               of all else.
It lasts, perhaps, an hour.

Afterwards,
Everything stands glass-glazed,
Stunned trembling.

You walk in the rainbowed world,
Feeling grass blades catch between your toes
And smelling what you don't know is ozone,
A little bit of heaven come down to call.

X. In the Attic

You sleep where only slanting slats and shingles
    Separate you from
        Sky.

Or do not sleep, but simply lie there and turn,
    As you know the stars, too, must turn,
        If you could see them.

The cottonwood scrapes at the roof like a claw,
    Like the cold hands
        Of the dead.

Your body can't seem to warm the quilts over you;
    You lie there, shivering,
        And turn . . .

Until what blooms behind your eyes betrays you,
    And you decide to give it up—
        Light the lamp.

It was long ago that you found, far back
    In the dresser, in a dark box,
        The photographs.

You get them out now and spread them in the closest
     Chronology you can contrive, then
          Put back all but three:

Your father, handsome, stands smiling by water
     In the south of France
          In 1945;

Your mother's face, beautiful and tinted rose,
     Floats up at you through the sepia
          Of its lost world;

And here is the aunt, also beautiful, whose love
     Came to a bad end having something
          To do with a gun,

And who is hardly ever spoken of, but who you
     Understand occupies a stark place
          In Hopkinsville.

You find it hard to say just what any of this
     Has to do with you,
          And yet

The stilled faces, caught both in and out of time, seem
     To require some nameless something of you.
          Near dawn,

You pour boiling water into a washtub and bathe,
     Then pee in the bathwater, humming
          A made-up tune.

XI. Your Shadow

The day your father dies,
It rains. You are mildly surprised
At how easily the world absorbs the blow,
How little there is to be done.

You bury him on a crisp afternoon
In the colored graveyard—because,
It turns out, that was his desire.
Thus, attendance is small.
For the kind, fat minister's Words,
You give him twenty dollars and a tight smile.

Sun has shocked the country
Into its final beauty of the year:
What leaves still hang hang in goldness
Against a liquid blue, and the fescue,
Swept with wind, shines its green—
The last green thing there is,
Save for some dark, sparse pines
In silhouette on the far ridge.

You linger a moment among flowers,
Then follow your shapely shadow back to the house.

You notice how good you look in black.

XII. The Monument

And so it always happens
That women, in half-lives,
Survive the ruined world
Men make and, ruining,

Leave:
      there is you,
And there is your mother,
Who remains only as a lightning-
Struck white oak remains
Standing gaunt on the hillside
Long after it's hollowed out.

And there is the aunt, and,
After three days of receiving
Farm wives who arrive with little
To say but much to eat,

You go to her,
         driving south-
Ward to Bowling Green, then
West on 68 through Auburn,
Russellville, Elkton. East
Of Hopkinsville, and taller
Than any silo in the country,

The Jefferson Davis Monument
Stands honing the pyramid
Of its pinnacle on blue air,
Looming there as if it could
Outlast the country itself.

XIII. At the Asylum

When the moon changes
On the east side of Hopkinsville,
Hardly human cries
Drift through the barred-over windows
Of a squat brick building.

Prison? No . . .
That other place—the one no one
        Says the name of,
Though the letters on the sign at the gate
        Are clearly legible:

WESTERN STATE HOSPITAL.
You tell them who you are, and they
        Let you through
To a circular driveway under grand oaks
        Bare with winter coming on,

        Shards of sky gone
The opaque gray of stone through the branches.
        You think the place smells
Like your old grade school, or the courthouse
        At Hardinburg,

        As you follow the sound
Of a nurse's rubber shoes down a corridor.
        The face
Is no worse than you expected, though you
        Expected the worst:

        Cheeks sagged
Like a scrotum, the mouth a wound
        Unhealing, with a half-
Mustache above it, and the eyes
        Pitch black, vision

        Turned inward
For . . . how many years now?
        And this the face
Of one who was once beautiful
        And who does not

        Recognize you now.
She'll tell you her story, though,

Which has no pattern
Or end, but goes on dawn to dark
        In babble-drool.

        It is the story
Of lovers, and a lost place and time,
        And a fall,
Which is only the oldest story there is,
        Which is your story,

        But which you cannot
Know the ending of till you've lived it,
        Or chosen not
To live it, or chosen her way,
        Which would be easy.

        You drive away
Through a tunnel your headlights make in the dark
        Toward a final darkness,
Which is the only place you've ever known,
        Which is home.

XIV. Intimate Variations

Listen: the wind is singing.
It is singing in the corrugated
Bark of a bare hickory,
In the gray woodwinds of grapevine,
In the rust softening the barbs
Of a sagging fencerow.

Listen: nothing. And yet
The utter soundlessness of things
Drawing constantly deeper

Into themselves can seem
The intensest of cries
To a young woman undressing—

Undressing, for no one, in an attic
Voluptuous with the scent
Of intimate variations
On a more common history—
Undressing simply to lie down
And let the dark undo her.

DAYS OF SUMMER GONE

*"was the saddest word of all there is nothing else in the
world its not despair until time its not even time until it was"*

—Faulkner, *The Sound and the Fury*

*"Me he puesto a recordar los
d'as de verano idos . . ."*

—César Vallejo, *Trilce*

Part One/ American Variations

The Distance

Two women are hugging each other goodbye
On the sidewalk in the tree-shadow
Of a late spring afternoon. It is not
Sexual, though both are beautiful.
And though both are tall and lithe
Under their dark hair, the differences
Between them are infinite
And support one another. Behind them,
In the distance, buildings
Tangential to the sun catch fire a moment,
Then darken. A young man, hands
In his pockets, is coming toward them.
The women are crying.
They are not yet ready to part.
And it is not sexual.
Even the young man, who is surely lonely,
Slows as he approaches them,
Feeling a sudden reverence
He wouldn't have thought himself capable of.
He stops half a block away.
The women part. They part
Like drapes drawn open
To catch the last light.
One of the women gets into a car
And drives away; the other
Waves, then turns back across the grass,
Perhaps to her apartment. And the young man
Walks on into the gathering
City twilight, which will be
More beautiful and lonely for him
When he looks up. His whole self is focused

On the precise spot of the women's
Parting. When he reaches the spot,
He stands there. Just stands there,
Transformed in the vivid air of their absence.

Party

Tonight, because they're not in jail, our downstairs neighbors
    Are having a party. Deep Purple
Seeps up through the floor, and if there were chandeliers,
    They'd be trembling like flowers in water.
In the white noise between songs, I can hear Ricardo Planas,
    Our fellow resident from El Salvador,
Cursing beautifully in Spanish. The guys downstairs,
    So far as we can tell, do nothing

Except get themselves arrested every week or so. I think
    They're dangerous, and you think
They just need to get laid. And, by god, they're trying.
    They hoot and whistle, trying to seduce
Coeds off the street, but the coeds aren't going for it,
    No matter how resourcefully their backsides
Are described. It's dusk, and it's soggy hot in here,
    So I decide to give up the literary life

For a gin and tonic and a view from the window.
    Over the building across the street
That used to be a grocery store that used to be
    A TV repair shop that used to be
A pet cemetery and which a young couple and their huge dog
    Have been trying to make into a home
For the past month, the sky is vaguely Turneresque
    Through a new green fleece of the willows.

The intensity of almost-summer is pulsing through the city
    Like heroin through the addict's veins,
The dog is sleeping to forget the weight of his chain,
    And the couple are enjoying their Cablevision.
Or maybe they're not. The woman stands in the doorway
    Contemplating the party downstairs, then,
Without explanation or goodbye to the man, comes striding
    Across the street to join it.

She is sadly pretty in her earth shoes and cut-offs
        And shirt that says she's a Pepper,
Her hair looking blown as if by some imaginary breeze.
        She can't be more than seventeen,
And the man, who can't be much more than that,
        Stands open-mouthed at the doorway.
"Victoria!" he screams, loud enough for me
        To hear it over the music.

"Where in the hell do you think you're going?"
        No answer I can make out.
"What in the hell are you doing to me, Victoria?"
        She's disappeared below the window.
"Goddamnit, Victoria! We're not talking about a relationship,
        We're talking about marriage!"
I'm embarrassed for him, and a little uneasy, and you
        Want to know what's going on.

"Do you love me, Victoria? Do you love me?"
        Apparently, she doesn't. He shakes
His fist at us or at the gods, then skulks back inside.
        I'm having visions of his returning
With a shotgun to blow away the guys downstairs,
        And perhaps me, too, and perhaps even
Ricardo Planas, who doesn't speak English well enough
        To debauch anybody's wife.

I glance at you and arch my eyebrows to suggest one last
        Sweaty quickie before I'm killed.
But when the guy comes back outside, he's still
        Barefoot, and armed only with a bottle
Of Jack Daniel's. He takes a long swig of bourbon,
        Then sits down on the sidewalk
And starts to cry, his bony chest heaving.
        I turn away. You've gone back

To the wild casserole you're concocting, and we
        Say nothing of what we've seen or heard

When I come back into the kitchen to pour myself another.
    I wander into the bedroom,
Light a cigarette, and lie down on the bare floor.
    The music throbs through me
Like an infection; the amber streetlights make
    Impossible maps on the walls.

A siren whines nearer and nearer, then fades away.
    The party will go on for hours,
Long past the time when sleep will seem our luxury.
    Maybe the young couple across the street
Will piece things back together; maybe Victoria
    Will ride west on a stolen motorcycle
With one of the guys downstairs and never be
    Heard from again; maybe her husband

Will hang himself to show her just how much
    He loves her. Maybe Ricardo Planas
Is thinking, this evening, of the beautiful woman
    He loved who was shot to death
For no reason on an otherwise quiet street in San Salvador.
    I don't know what any of it means or matters.
In the morning, sure as sunrise, we'll all dress our bodies
    And walk out hungover into America.

American Variations

I. Lost Winter Seascape with Figures

Once there was a world you could
Hold in the palm of your hand,
And upon which the snow was
Always just starting to fall—

World of a city that lay
By a body of water
Where people gathered to watch
Ships set sail for other worlds.

And high over the city
At the edge of the water,
Stood a great woman of stone
Whose name no one remembers.

Once there was a world you could
Hold in the palm of your hand,
And, by turning it over,
Make the first soft snow swirl down

On the lit houses of those
Whose name no one remembers,
But who, it seems now, must have
Loved one another greatly.

Why else would they have taken
The trouble to put her there—
Stone woman who stood waiting
For ships that never came back?

II. Song to Be Spoken, Not Sung

Say *snow drifting through some small town at dusk,*
And listen to the syllables die in your bare room
Like snow drifting through some small town at dusk.

Say *Fall, rain!* as the rain falls down on you
But know it would have fallen anyway.

Say *this world* and let it be enough, for once.

Say the drunk dancing in the middle of the intersection
At three in the morning didn't have to go on
Turning green, then yellow, then red, then green again.

Say you didn't have to feel the one you love
Grow distant in the parentheses of your arms.

Say *this life* and let it be enough, for once.

III. The Woman with the Blue Bandana

Just across the river from Indiana
Are a farm and a woman I once loved.
I wanted to go West, and the woman waved
Goodbye to me, from a field, with a blue bandana.

I made it as far as Texarkana,
Where, lonely, every night I remembered
How gold the fields of the farm got in September,
And how the woman let her hair loose from the blue bandana.

Just across the river from Indiana,
That farm's fields have gone fallow since,
And the woman lies unmoving, unmoved, who once
Wiped clean the white bed of our love with her blue bandana.

IV. The Return

And when, finally, you found your way back,
It seemed you barely recognized the place—
Or rather, the place barely recognized you.

The great rivers (Cumberland, Tennessee)
Rolled on as always; cardinals and jays
Skirmished among the crosses of dogwood.

But visiting friends, their faces both the same
And not the same, you realized how the loss
Of a common language could undo the world:

How the sky over each landscape contained
The blueprints of a city that might rise
When all your generation had gone away,

And how lovers were, in the end, reduced
To the sounds of names, the flesh utterly forgotten.
And it seemed then that you'd come all this way

Only to pass unnoticed through the place,
Driving fast down dangerous, familiar roads
Like a shadow you had cast years before.

V. At Equinox

Far from the sea, a field
Of flowers makes a sort of sea;
And here in the city, far from fields,
The sky makes a field as blue as sea.

And, too, from time to time, a man
And a woman agreeing, lie curled
To make what little love they can
In this, their one and only world.

Your Sex

I think about your sex.
My heart simplified, I think about your sex,
As the hind flank of the day ripens.
I press the button for good luck; I touch the bud
Of happiness—it's in season.
And whatever grief I might have felt before
Simply dies inside me.

I think about your sex, that sweet furrow,
Womb-shadow of harmony,
Though there's no denying that death
Exists in the same world.
Sometimes I think it's best just to take pleasure
Wherever we want and can.
Look: the twilight is alive with wild honey.

The Name of Desire

The Holiday Inn Vanderbilt, Nashville

After the many-colored but mostly blue
Seasons of our two solitudes—the hours
Of longing and the flight from longing, the years
Spent remembering as if memory were true—
We stand together on a balcony
Above the city of losses, the city of lights
Bouncing back off a starless sky, the city
Where we'll try to save this night from the death of nights.
Ours has become a life in which the self
And the self's other begin to anticipate the chances
Taken in the name of desire. Desire:
That sweet song the body sings to itself,
Or under the best of circumstances
The song two bodies sing to each other.

A Hymn to the Body

Because summer persists longer
In my city than yours—
Chill mornings, but the sky at dusk
Still lingering in the diminishing exchange
Of light and dark—
I've not stopped remembering your dream
Of beautiful women riding white horses
Across a field of dew,
And what you'd woken from the dream
To witness the morning your call came.
I never thought to ask
Why it was me you chose to phone—a lover
Already falling from your good favor,
As if the seven blocks between us then
Had grown gradually significant—
And it didn't much matter,
As I followed the increasingly urgent
Modulations in your voice
When you left off telling the dream to describe
The abstracted shape of a body
Below the window, stone-still among the strewn shards
Of the motorcycle he'd flown in a sickening
Two-hundred-foot arc
From the freeway overpass to your front lawn.
And before the rising of the sun,
Before your waking and witnessing,
There was nothing that stranger's body could do
But cool and go pale,
As if absorbing starlight;
And nothing you could do, having seen,
But keep superfluous watch
Over the torn leather torso and broken legs,
Hugging yourself through the camisole
Till the cops arrived

To ask the usual questions and clear the yard.
That night, as we lay
Murdering a bottle of Blanc de Blancs
In a dimmed hotel room high above the city,
We talked about the body:
I of its profusion of sculptural form,
And you of the tenuous suturing
By which it holds to this life.
Lying there, listening
To the slow swish of traffic after rain,
I understood what it was we'd given up
By learning to live in cities,
And why, under such circumstances,
One might be led to dream
Of white horses in a field of dew,
Or simply of horses,
Of a field of dew.
And lying there, studying our timed breath
Made tangible with cigarettes,
I understood how the frail and intricate grace
Of a mare's fetlock might be thought
Divine, and how some shiftless gambler,
Unshaven, forlorn by numbers,
And losing the last of the money
That wasn't his to lose
As that mare pulls away in the final furlong,
Might be saved by the mere
Beauty of the thing, and, before turning
Away, let his shot eyes bathe
In the almost-too-much green of the infield.
And if I believed, for a moment, that our bodies
Were numinous beyond whatever might
Outlast us, whatever might someday begin
To shine in an austere clarity
For no one—
And if I told myself that shining
Mattered less than the slightest thing
I could touch,

Then it was a sin
For which I do not ask to be forgiven—
Not even now, as summer falters,
And you and I get on with the very different
Businesses of our lives in separate cities,
And the heart no longer especially cares
To catch the final nuances
Of a music that sustained it once.
Already I'm probably betraying it, remembering it wrong,
But what mattered was not, finally, your dream
Of women on horseback,
Or the stranger's body cast down like a twisted
Sentence some god couldn't bring himself
To complete, or even
The quiet, strained love we made.
It was the way a slowly revolving disc
Of light from the airfield halfway across town
Silhouetted in silver the almost imperceptible
Cilia of down along the undersides
Of your drawn thighs—
And when the sun, slipping
Behind a staggered row of pines
In northern Mississippi or Tennessee
In late August,
Hangs the needles in its distant, momentary fire,
Then lets them go,
And the bickering cries of the gathering starlings
Rise in praise of the falling dark.

The Story

If it rained tonight
    I'd lie down
For a thousand years.

—As if nothing had happened;
    As if the story
Wouldn't retell itself forever:

No more mother, no remembered loves, and my pulse
    Purified, the only sound
As I lowered myself into the depths. . . .

But the bells are ringing up the hill,
    Punishing bells,
Recounting all the arguments against me.

If I've created the story of my life,
    Why not now the story
Of not having ever lived at all?

Maybe then there wouldn't be this burden
    Of what was lost
Almost before it had arrived.

Maybe then there wouldn't be this weight
    Of what is
And what I can feel myself already losing.

Black Water

It happens like this
    Over and over:
A light breaks on the shore
    Of a black water
Hemmed in by cliffs of red
    Stone with faces
Carved into the faces, and you
    See another face
—The face of the remembered—
    Rising from the water,
Descending from the sourceless light,
    And cannot call it out,
Because now you are the light breaking
    Over the black water,
And you are the black water, and you
    Are the face they make.

And then you wake up, and light
    A cigarette,
And you are in time again, the world
    Of time and outside
It is Tuesday, and early June,
    And 1985.
And it would be your wedding day,
    Were it three years ago;
And it would be your anniversary
    Had she not left you . . .
But it is simply a Tuesday, in June,
    In 1985,
And you have woken up alone to the life
    You live alone,
And the workmen down the block are hammering
    The last of the dream from you.

And what work will there be
.....For you today,
Dreamer whose dream the world
.....Of time has torn away?
—What task to occupy your hands
.....That tremble?
Only this resurrection of the grief
.....That sweats the drink
Out of you and makes you thirst
.....For more—
Makes you dress up to go out and drink,
.....Then undress to lie down.
And you will lie down, and you will be
.....The light breaking
Over the black water, and you will be
.....The black water.

Autumn Fugue

I remember how the silver leaves fell down,
Extravagantly, as if in prefigured spirals,
From the fig tree you couldn't keep alive,
And how, when you'd sat watching for a while
That lovely dying, then turned your face to me,
Your face seemed the same silver of the leaves.

It had to do partially, I suppose,
With the light—how the brief and intense dusk
Along 14th Street gathered in the canopy
Of chestnuts choked with vine, filtering
In through the three windows of your white room
To make a luminous lake in which we swam.

Looking all that autumn for a holier way
Of talking about things, you found yourself
Hardly able, at last, to speak at all;
And so, for long moments, no word would pass
Between us, when we had only to listen
To the quarter-hourly noise from a nearby church.

There was something greater to the sadness
Than simply the going away of your lover,
Or even our own past failure at love.
What sadness there was carried with it the weight
Of something intensely formal, and which would not
Be overcome by anything so commonplace

As a gesture shared between the two of us.
And so, as the light faltered and the leaves fell down,
I'd light a cigarette and sip my drink,
And you'd arrange your body at the window
Like some unfinished portrait of yourself. . . .
If there is nothing between a man and a woman

Except the light by which they see each other,
And a past in which they appear continually smaller,
And a future that seems already to have acquired
The irrevocability of the past,
It seems important, nevertheless, to acknowledge
Their brief victory: the surviving it.

Plain Talk

Beyond the I-feel-you-feel-
We-feel of our psychoanalyzed lives,
It is summer.

Later,
Maybe we'll part, but for now
There's supper to fix and no anxiety
In your brown legs.
Moosehead
Is not an unnatural act with a large northern animal,
Though I have seen suspect red panties draped across the racks
Of dead ones.
Once,
Trying to grow a slender tail of hair on my neck,
I told my skinny-beautiful barberess to "accentuate" it,
Who cut it off.
When I think
Of that lock lying there like a severed little finger,
Of how much I already missed it, I remember remember
remember
To always talk plain.

The Seasons: A Quartet

I

Come late autumn, I'll wear black leather again,
My gray felt boots make a sound like the perfect crime
As I pass along the deserted avenue
Some Sunday evening, admiring the dried-up fountains.

I think the trees will be left harsh and bare
As Donatello's *Mary Magdalene*:
Their branches thorns, their leaves fallen hair.
And you? You'll know it's finally a fine line

We walk between the last fall and the next,
And a faith without foundation by which we survive
Such seasons as these. Look at the washed-out sky,
At the stars competing with streetlamps, then look for me:

I'll be the stranger slouching on the corner,
His face lit by a dying match. I'll be
Everything you've tried not to remember,
But which is reflected in the half-light of your eyes.

II

Is this the Russian snow Napoleon's legions
Bloodied with their feet before they fell?
No, just sundown in Paducah, Kentucky,
Day's last shallow breath shading to a faint rose

The soft white other side of the river.
I seem to remember turning away, once,
From this same balcony with its twisted railing
Dense as a frozen black gum, to see you

Still sewn up in your warm dream, till my breath
Frosted the glass over. Now, as tugboats slice
Their way through the ice on the Ohio again,
I think the *Belle of Louisville* has gone down

To winter in New Orleans, and I wonder
About the why and wherefore of your departure.
It's cold out here, and this feeble light won't last
The time it will take me to drink it a silent toast.

III

So the rain falls, and the garden grows full
Of itself, fruits and flowers like brushstrokes
Against the lush dark backdrop of the woods.
Somewhere in the woods a stream is playing

Lightly as some old desire turned inward,
And somewhere in the stream a single sunfish
Lets its flat side break the pane of water
At an isolate oval of light in the dense cathedral.

All is desire: hushed lull before the storm,
Rain like scythes through the fields, scattered birds
Breaking into song to find one another,
The coming dark's duet of moon and star.

Five summers ago, I watched a woman
Wander into the garden at dusk, select
A tomato, and close her eyes as the juice fell
Like something utterly pure onto her breasts.

IV

What Pasternak called "Unforgetting September"
Ripens as always, and Tchaikovsky's Hunting Party,
Lured too far into the forest by the red fox,
Is lost forever. I am listening

To the String Quartet No. 1 in D Major
With its heartbreaking second movement Tolstoy
Wept through in Moscow in 1871.
(Tchaikovsky got the theme from a gardener.)

I can remember as well as September does,
And what music remains inside of me
Is muted over with memory, strains sad
As the seed that spills from the withered okra plants.

The best days of summer are the days of summer gone:
Something cooking, a wash of light on the water. . . .
The music dies, and what I hold is the world.
One leaf falling would break the spell. It falls.

Part Two / Speaking of the South

Speaking of the South: 1961

John F. Kennedy is alive and loved, and the moon remains
Somewhat of a mystery, and suburbs and shopping malls

Are mainly somebody's bad ideas, and you can still
Speak of the South in a voice not wholly laden with loss.

In Cadiz, Kentucky, my father pastors a Baptist church;
My mother types up his sermons, visits the town's sick.

Later, he'll leave the ministry to sell stocks and bonds,
And she'll leave him for a journalist from Birmingham.

Kennedy will be shot. People will yawn at the conquered moon.
The South will sprout suburbs and shopping malls like tubercles.

But for now, say it's December in Cadiz, Kentucky.
Tinsel for Christmas drapes Main Street, flickering

As dusk comes on cold with a blue wind off Lake Barkley.
The poolroom and diner fill with smoke and the low voices

Of men who carry inside them the stillness of the fields
They hope to work for at least another twenty-five years.

A boy kisses his girl goodbye and follows his visible breath
Home, dreaming of her creamy thighs and a red Chevrolet.

In the Wishy-Washy, the divorcee folds her stained whites.
And in a yellow room of the Trigg County Hospital,

I am born—not yet named, nor equipped with the facility
Of language, but squalling even then to make myself heard.

In Search of the Other World

And the dead—
What time are they due back?
The autumn dusk of Houston announces itself
In streetlights the color of melons.

As a child, I'd sit on my mother's haunches
While she lay on her stomach with her bra undone,
And rub her back in exchange for stories
Of her childhood in Elkton, Kentucky.
I didn't understand, at the time, that most of the people
She spoke of had long since died.
That other world we entered with our eyes closed
And my hands making invisible figures on her shoulders
Seemed real to me. For years
I expected to meet her alcoholic father
Who threw the farm away giving summer picnics.
(Done in the high Southern style,
They were the talk of all Todd County.)
Or Homer, the druggist, who danced
Formal waltzes with an imaginary woman
While he mixed up cherry sodas.
Or C.C. and Jim, the elderly black couple
Who walked two miles into town each Saturday night
Merely for music and ice cream.
Later, when I asked her if she believed in God,
She said, "I guess."

As a child, I'd lead my friends to the edge of the suburbs
Where we built tree houses, dammed up ravines,
Or imitated in half-finished duplexes the lives of adults.
Those days were holy, if anything ever was.
And those friends' names, when I say them to myself,
Sound numinous even now:
Rhonda, Jeffry, Timothy, Star.
I think they must still be waiting for me

To finish supper so we can make one last foray
Into a field outside Winchester.
They're waiting for me because they,
Like the dead my mother conjured
As my hands passed along her ribs,
Have no other recourse:
                              The future
Turned out to be little consolation
For those chill Kentucky twilights
When our every parting seemed final.

Rhonda, Jeffry, Timothy, Star?
I call out, walking strange streets,
Searching at random in the darkness.

And though I know it's useless to look for them
Among the four million of Houston,
I can't believe they'd leave me
To face such a life as this.

Ode to a Relative I Never Met

1

So this is where that enigma of a great-uncle
Painted the pictures no one will remember.
I stand a long time, hands in my pockets,
Slow breath scoring the noon winter air,
Gazing dumbly into the spare, harsh woods
It seems he hated so much he felt compelled
To refashion them on canvas after canvas.

2

He was seldom spoken of in our house:
Touched, not of this world—words that nurtured
A grotesque fear in the mind of the child
They were designed to pacify. Each Christmastime
The postman—ruddy-cheeked, his blue uniform
Flecked with the season's first snow—would deliver
A flat, square package, which my father opened
In disgusted silence and later burned out back.
Always those same woods, each year a little darker;
Always that same smoke rising toward nothing.

3

Tonight, tired of the fire, tired of its light,
Its warmth, I'll wrap my yearning body and walk out.
—Submit myself to the starless dark's instruction,
To the cold encroachment of those all-but-invisible woods.

In Atlanta Once

In Atlanta once, on Peachtree Street,
I met a woman and took her in my arms,
Lifting her body to see the blond fire
Of her hair flare against buildings, sky.

The woman was my cousin, but there was more
To it than that—or should have been,
Though I doubt she remembered.
And even I, standing there, could think
Of little except the word *horse*, and the way
We'd used that word in a childhood game,
And what the letter *h* had signified.

She was married. Married,
After what we did as children
In the house of an aunt now dead.

It's always dusk when I pass through Atlanta,
And into that insouciant summer dusk
I let her go.
                    Later, caught in traffic,
I saw jets drift over, huge,
Lights flashing in first dark.

Across the latitudes of afternoons and years,
From some nameless room, I felt a quavering.
It was nothing. It was the place of true desire:
Playing Doctor, playing Horse . . . but everything
Tricked away, now, from that purity.

Yes, cousin. Live your life.

Loca Sancta

That field I floated Shelly Solare's panties into,
Summer of 1979, their frail lace hung
In moonlight forever above the dark rows of corn.

Fathers and Sons

*"But the sultriness of noonday passes, and evening comes, and
night, and then, too, the return to a calm haven, where sleep is
sweet for the tortured and the weary. . . ."*

—Turgenev

In my father's recurring dream,
His life's humiliations take on the form
Of a procession of slow-drawn, open boxcars.
A hideous old man hangs out by one arm
From each of them, his blackened face leering.

It's late winter as he tells me this.
We're sitting on the back porch, sipping beers,
Watching the dusk play itself out
In a lightshow through the woods,
Shocked yellows and reds blazing the leaf rot

Where the neighbors' son lay down and
Shot himself last October, the note stuffed
In his shirt pocket: *Pretty place
To die.* They've moved away now,
Their house empty and up for sale.

A train sounds in the distance, pure sound,
Its fading whines and shudders dragging off
What's left of the light, while my breath
And the stars my breath rises to meet
Become visible against the dark.

And this evening I understand
What little consolation stars are—
How their shimmering is out of reach
As the smooth stones or the small fish flashing
In a frozen-over stream, and how my father,

Staring up at them, can only think
How alone he is out here, among these wasted

Fields the woods are reclaiming year by year.
"It's terrible, just terrible," he says,
Meaning his dream. "It goes on forever,

And there's nothing I can do to stop it."
And we can't help each other, he and I.
We've perfected our obsessions and traveled
Too far into ourselves, like the mystic
Made ashes by his own imploding light.

After Rain

Steam rises from the tapeworm road like dust
Raised by the wagons of the dead,

And my sad father, whose eyes won't latch
Onto anything for long anymore,

Is already worrying at the rust
Still yet to form on things left out.

The rain has plumped the corn up just enough
For the raccoons to pillage it tonight,

Waddling through the dark to climb the stalks
And ride the finest ears earthward.

In the morning my father will stand
Mute under a mute sky, beside what only yesterday

Was his garden, and think, "Well, anyway,
There are the flowers," and kneel down

With a faith that has outlasted
Faith, trying to salvage what he can.

Three Scenes from the Provinces of Blood

1

In your mother's kitchen, I can manage
    My world.
In your mother's kitchen, on a summer
    Sunday morning, I write:
"In your mother's kitchen, I can manage
    My world."
And test the idea against a vase
    Of wild geraniums
On the windowsill. The glass is so old
    It's *slud*
(As Dizzy Dean would have said), warped
    Like a thin
Slow river, the landscape it frames
    Coming through in waves.
And the flowers, because they don't know
    They're beautiful,
And because, soon, they won't be, are
    Beautiful, and today,
In your mother's kitchen, are a part
    Of the world I can manage.

2

I remember rolling the window down just outside
    Cadiz, Kentucky,
And feeling the air thick and fragrant
    As a woman in summer
Rush through the car as the car rushed
    Further into summer,
Past fields long abandoned to flowers
    And weeds, past stands
Of cottonwood and pine and beech with pieces

Of washed sky sticking through,
Past mansions and trailer parks and billboards
    For MARLBORO and EARLY TIMES,
And being suddenly overcome by a longing
    For what I couldn't name,
And trying to reconstruct from memory
    My father's lonesome face,
And not being able to for the changing landscape,
    Then finding that face as the car
Arched skyward onto the bridge over Lake Barkley,
    Then losing it in the fire on the water.

3

What I remember of that summer
    Is the trying
Not to remember—giving myself over
    To the taste and smell
Of things: sassafras, honeysuckle,
    Earth's bittersweets.
What I remember is the cacophony
    Of bugs and birds,
And nodding flowers filmed with dust,
    And wooden walls gone gray,
And the countryside composing itself each dawn,
    Dissolving again each dusk.
I remember my grandmother trying to kindle
    Life between the cupped hands
Of work, while my grandfather was trying
    To die.
And I remember the dream that never would
    Let me sleep:
I was walking on bloody bare feet down a dark
    Gravel road to nowhere.

A Wreath of Stars:
Symsonia, Kentucky, 1914

They'd caught me skimming cream off the top of the churn,
So half that winter I had to go upstairs
Right after supper without any dessert—
No thick-comb honey Mamie stored in jars.

No muscadine, no sunset-colored cake
Sweetened with molasses, no piecrust plumped
With apple or blackberry. Still, what made me ache
The most was missing that music my brother thumped

Out on his guitar while Pap's fiddle whined
Along like some hurt thing—like the bitch retriever
Hung up in barbed wire for hours, who tried
To eat me alive when I came to uncut her.

I'd climb those stairs like somebody going to heaven
Before he was ready, the loose boards creaking, then breathe
On my frosted-over window till seven
Cold stars shone on the dark sky in a wreath.

                    *

The night Pap and my brother didn't come in
For supper, Mamie told me to go ahead
And eat their peach cobbler. We waited, then—
I watching through my window while she read.

And along towards midnight I saw two figures weaving
Down the road: one tall and lean, the other
Much the same, singing and carefully passing
A thick glass jug between them—Pap and my brother.

They must have saved a month to buy that whiskey.
But leaning together, their sweet breath rising like clouds,
One passed the jug, the other didn't see,
And the glass broke open on the frozen ground.

They stared down at the spill as at a grave,
Then at each other—with hatred for a minute;
Then knelt down as though praying to be saved
And lapped up every star reflected in it.

Part Three/ One World

Study

A ruined garden between ruined walls,
October, late sun bright on dry grass,
And wind sifting through leaves high overhead.
The light smells faintly of a river
And touches Ann's blond hair as it touches grass,
As light and wind touch the leaves.

The river is a block from here.
She feels it the same way she feels the pulse
Of blood beneath her skin. Crossing her legs
On the stone bench, she smoothes her skirt
And gazes up at the blue sky
Where it could almost still be summer.

But the wind shakes leaves loose now and then,
The leaves are brown, and migratory birds
Beat southward. Southward, too, Ann's lover,
Back to his city. In the garden,
Statues of lovers lie in shards
By crumbling brick where lovers used to walk.

She remembers how the light looked on the water
When they walked down by the river summer nights,
How the wind from the water touched her hair.
She'd go there now, but the day is late.
It's too far, that one block down to the river,
Where it must still be summer, even now.

Bored Cop Leaning against Abstract
Sculpture on Plaza below Skyscraper

There's little doubt the artist would be pleased
To see him leaning here loafing, fifty,
Balding and overweight, by tiny trees
The sun can't touch for the buildings of the city.
He scuffs one big black shoe on the concrete,
Looks up like an aging outfielder shagging
A fly, then turns his attention to his beat,
Where expensively dressed women walk wagging
Shopping bags. For years now, there's been no mention
Of promotion, and his youth's a played-out song.
He strokes the sculpture, dreaming of his pension.
The day is late, and he's tired, but however long
It takes for something to happen, he can wait . . .
—Then reach for the billyclub, the thirty-eight.

The Blue World

The two figures are lying fully clothed
On separate beds and staring at the ceiling
As if they could see the sky through the five
Stories above them. It is dusk, and, caught
In the blue world Matisse loved, refracted
Bars of late light ordering their bodies like
Keyboards, these strangers—this man and woman—
Have forgotten the name of the city
Outside and cannot think of anything
They want. He begins to smoke, and the woman,
Who doesn't smoke, watches the tracery
Of his breath rising and lets her mind drift
With it, as if seeing herself from above.
She feels that nothing will ever happen
To her and wonders how for years her life
Has gone on and gone on like somebody
Else's dreaming, how little it has to do
With her anymore. Then quietly, as though
His voice had come back to him suddenly,
Strange from disuse, the man begins speaking
Just to hear himself speak. The woman shifts
Imperceptibly on the cool mattress to listen,
Though the glib words she hears may as well be
Meaningless, or of another language.
She is thinking of music, of how much
Like music this man's voice is—perhaps
Because the sky is emptying itself
Like the chord dying inside a guitar,
Or because the frail notes of the streetlamps
Seem to echo the stars. And it is like
Matisse's *Piano Lesson*—this room,
This lopsided duet half-drowned in deep
Blue shade: the boy, bolt upright, practicing
The *Bagatelles*, maybe; the stern mother

Tricked into forgetting, for a moment,
Life's cruelty; the city reduced to a source
Of light through the bay window; the pendulum
Of the metronome hung forever between beats.

Photograph: *Being Sad*
(an early self-portrait with freckles)

I suppose I should begin by saying
I once made love to this woman,
Though the black and white image,
Faded a bit on the thick, warped paper,
Doesn't remember her body as my body

Remembers it. And, too, because
The camera was tilted slightly,
The angles of the room behind her—
That same bedroom, walled with books—
Fall strangely away, disturbing me.

She dons a white slip, paints her face
Even paler than usual, balances
The Nikon on the chair, and, crouching,
Brings the calculatedly disheveled
Empty bed almost into focus.

Then sets the timer and plunges
Into a grief that doesn't look feigned
Because it's not.—Just lying there,
Drawn so tightly into her own arms
As after making love which is not love.

Two Anonymous Spanish Drawings

1

Approaching the place from above—mountain
Behind and plain spreading seaward before—
You see the town reflected in its fountain
And have the feeling there is something more
That has to do with you here than meets the eye.
Arches and columns lift up like images torn
From memory; churches steeple the sky.
It occurs to you: this is where you were born.
And it is at once familiar and strange,
How the people gathered round the huge urn
On the plaza act as if nothing has changed,
How they seem to have anticipated your return—
Though you can never hope to wholly survive
In this land where you continually arrive.

2

Early in the morning on the narrow street,
You see, walking toward you, a woman,
And another woman walking away. From the sky,
The sunlight angles halfway down the walls
Of tall houses to your right, while balconies
To the left of you remain in the cool of the shadow.

You are able to make out the V-shaped shadows
Of pigeons that lifted from eaves high up on the walls
And flew straight out of the picture, into the sky.
Risen sleepers stand yawning on the balconies.
They lean there, looking down onto the street,
Where, because it is morning, the two women

Are hurrying to where they have to be. The woman
Coming toward you walks close to the left wall,
As if to avoid you and remain in shadow;
The other is already too far down the street
For you to catch her or call out. The balconies
Would be bright with summer flowers, and the sky

Would be the deep blue appropriate for summer skies,
Had the artist bothered to color them in. The walls
Would be yellow and beige, though mauve where shadows
Are still lingering along the little street.
You must imagine the colors of the dresses the women
Wear, and can only surmise that, behind an empty balcony,

Two lovers lie coupling, taking care that the balcony
Drapes are drawn. When they finish, the woman
Will wash herself over a basin the color of the sky,
Open the drapes to erase the room of shadows,
And watch the man make his way down the street,
His familiar whistling echoing off the walls.

Farther down, the street curves between the close walls,
And a steeple the shape of a pencil scrapes the sky.
You'll never see the view from those far balconies,
Nor know what might lie hidden there in shadow,
Nor catch the attention of these two women.
You'll simply have to stand here in the street,

Dreaming of other women behind the walls,
Wondering how the sky might look from the balconies
When the shadows of evening fall on the narrow street.

Contemplating a Landscape in Spring

As if the forms were
Already etched there
On the bare canvas,
You frown at color,
Waiting for the light
To correct itself.

Or is it summer
You're waiting for now,
That recurring dream
Of final ripeness
From which each summer
Is a falling off?

Each way the light falls
Is a falling off:
The sun slants too low;
Clouds that were just right
A moment ago
Are already gone;

And as the frail brush-
Strokes passing birds make
Fade, so memory
Of them fades, until
The sky itself, for
All its blue, seems blank.

The wounds of winter
Bother you, but there's
No wound a brushstroke
Wouldn't heal, or which
Might not find a place
In the finished work.

Spring's a becoming,
Process as product,
A *was* almost *is*.
Say the dogwood's shy,
And that the grapevine
Dreams it's full of wine.

Against the bare field,
Below the dark line
Of the distant hills,
Even the birdbath's
Soiled decadence
Has a sort of charm.

Tell me: isn't there
A chance it's we who
Require revision?
How green do the grass,
The trees have to get
Before you begin?

Two Songs of Solitude and Lament

1

There's nothing to celebrate this evening.
      I've come home tired
To a mailbox gorged with junk it can't
      Digest, to a room bereft
Of any hope of getting put into order,
      To a radio gone numb
With humming the old tunes and passing along
      The old gossip: a breakthrough,
A disaster, the economy's rise or fall, a war
      Going on somewhere.

No one will come by, no one will call,
      No ex-friend or -lover
Materialize from my wired-out memory.
      Boredom is dangerous:
It gets easier with practice. The streetlights,
      As if in celebration
Of nothing, erupt the off-shade of cheap champagne,
      While in the bedroom
The clock I can never think to wind
      Ticks down like a bomb.

2

Dozing to the tugging drone of fans
      These summer afternoons,
The haunt of memory surrounds and inhabits me
      Like a siege on some ruined city.
Runners of sunlight manage to twist their way
      Through a full-leafed maple,
And the shadow-splotched walls of this room are suddenly
      The blush of blood

Across the skin above your breasts
    When you came.
Or it rains, and everything the rain streams down
    Remembers your hair.
We were in each other's arms then, but now
    We are in the arms of the wind.
The proud ancient warriors, in hopeless bondage,
    Would kill themselves
By biting their tongues in two, so as to bleed to death.
    I wake in the dark
And walk out onto the balcony to watch the stars
    That won't touch down on the rooftops.

Weightlifter Poems

1. Tao of the Weightlifter

Musculature as a way of life.
Breaking it down to build it.
Up. A burning in my shoulders.

—As if I were beginning to sprout
Wings, but did not yet understand
The aesthetics of flight.

2. The Weightlifter in America

Christ, I should be in magazines!
—The way my oiled body can hardly
Contain itself, the way it looms
In the mirror like a glossy page!

3. The Weightlifter Dreaming of Women

All night the traffic's headlights
Throw tangled shadows across the walls of my room.
It is within this splotched cage
I turn and turn in sleep.

Though I never see her face
                          she speaks to me.

All night the factories
Float up their thick white smoke
Which fuels the stars
Which also turn.

If I press too hard against her

she is gone.

Waking in the dustlight of morning's noise,
I reach out and crush air between my heavy arms—
Till, anchored again in my body, I walk away
From the angel of sweat on the mattress.

And though I cannot lift her

she will rise.

4. *The Weightlifter's Tug of War*

Six a.m., and already I've started
Sweating again. Last night's rain
Just steamed things up a little more.

All summer staring out this huge window,
And still I can't name the tree across the street.
It has climbed itself upward, path of least resistance.

Shafts of light flash between buildings. Grim faces
Of workmen in sharp relief. Along the sidewalk
Dappled with shadows, a white rope inches toward me.

Two women are holding the ends of the rope.
Between them, eight children in bright clothes
Are tethered to it by their little hands.

I think this is so they won't be lost. I want them
To throw the rope up to me, but they don't see me.
I would raise them so gently, one at a time.

5. The Weightlifter Imagines His Death

Not of cancer, not of old age,
But suddenly—
As when the bar slips
And the iron comes crashing through my chest
Like the shrunken planet through some unlucky ceiling.

And I will be the man
No one remembers,
Who won't be able to tell them—
Even if he knew—whether it's worth,
After all, the strength it takes to carry on.

Lament on New Year's Day

I used to stroll untroubled down the variegated street,
The street I knew as I knew my own mind,
Where everything was real and without novelty.
And giving myself away to the depths of things,
I was gone.

Later, I doubled back down that same street,
Perhaps hoping to find the past lurking
In that wound of a room we'd shared
In the house on the corner.
And it was as if nothing had happened
In the years since her leaving.

Still, they don't come back, the great days,
The cries clarified with distance,
The fragrant lining of a patent leather shoe
Already beautiful beyond its function.

There was a precise moment towards dusk
When the window of a certain room was ringed with light,
And the dark walnut of an antique desk proclaimed
That those who were able to save themselves
Would be twice reimbursed tomorrow for their suffering.

Now, a V-shape of migrating geese
Or bombers on a practice mission
Freezes in mid-flight and turns to blue ash
In the sky above 1986.

The Changes

Dear Frank,

I'm nursing my hangover with coffee and chili and ice water
At Carol's Kitchen on Shepherd.
The place has that Southern feel I miss:
Plate lunch special, film of grease on the booths,
All the waitresses mothers or bitches.
I'd bet money none of them has been fucked since 1965.

Outside, it's Saturday and overcast,
The street gray but for the occasional yellow or wine
Of a tree beginning to turn.
I can forget my body in my brief astonishment
At autumn's having finally reached Houston.

Yesterday, my brave maroon Matador faltered.
Two women drove up in a wrecker to tow it away.
Smoke was still seeping out from under the hood,
And there was a little green river of radiator fluid.
(Some deep implosion of the steel *cojones*, I understand.
I doubt it will ever be the same again.)
So took Metro downtown, riding beside a Chicano girl
Who smelled like gardenias and whose thigh bumped into mine
    at the stops.

Main Street was luxuriant with the cold fire of afternoon,
And it seemed to me the winos were dreaming
Rivers at the ends of blocks.
Pondering the big gaudy Miró sculpture as dusk came on—

Skyscrapers lighting up against a starless pale mauve—
I thought of poor James Wright:
The needle they stuck between his ribs to drain the lungs,
His refusal to die in Minneapolis,
How much he loved the drowned whore.
I ended up getting drunk in La Carafe
And having to call a woman to come rescue me.
Christ, Frank, what would we do without women?

And why is it so hard to ever tell the truth about the past?
All morning, off and on, I've been staring at a photograph
Of the Scott Fitzgeralds taken in Paris in the Twenties.
Scott's face looks chiseled out under the cheekbones
And under the eyes, though the eyes themselves still dazzle.
The work isn't coming so easily now,
And he has begun to drink.
Beside him, Zelda—mad, beautiful Zelda—
Stares over my shoulder into some other world
From under her extravagant hat.

                    My first affair
Was with a woman who wore such a hat:
Black satin, with a slender, turned-down brim
And a single gray feather held by a pearl pin.
Betraying my wife and, later, betraying her,
Marked the beginning of my slow exile from Bowling Green.
I never knew what happened to her after that,
But you might have seen her on the street some afternoon
And remarked at the almost luminous whiteness of her face.
It occurs to me that, on Saturdays in autumn,
She liked to take a thermos of hot buttered rum
To the downtown square and stroll on bare, numb feet
Among the statues she imagined she resembled.

The changes, Frank, the changes.
Here, I do a job; I survive the city
By giving myself over to its beauty only from a distance.
And I've tried to learn to love only so far

As that love is specific and precise,
And to leave when I feel it becoming otherwise.
But sometimes, when I'm holding a woman in the dark,
A siren oscillates out on the street,
And something nameless shudders through me, tempting me
To make the connections that can undo a life.

And, too, one remembers so much—
Especially now, when the trees turn and the rains begin,
And the failing light makes the days ahead
Seem like so many pages on which nothing will be written,
And you can feel each moment, as it passes,
Transforming itself into one small, bright stone
In the huge and forever-unfinished mosaic
Of all that is lost.

Days of Summer Gone

It's too late to go back to that apartment
In Bowling Green, Kentucky, where we slept together
So many nights. I wonder if whoever lives there now
And fucks in that bed ever wonders about us?

If memory's any good gauge, the place
Must be ghosted with us even now—
Where I read aloud to you the love stories
Of other languages, and where there was no part
Of your body my tongue couldn't locate in the dark.
Don't try to tell me you've forgotten.

I can't let them go, those days
Of summer gone, for under my eyelids you move
As you moved through the changes of light in that room.

But it's raining tonight
In Houston, Texas, and how is your weather
In Berkeley? What happened to us?
Westward is the world's motion, and time's,
If not memory's.

One World

I have a photograph:
It is the green of a Kentucky summer,
A few skinny sycamores
Gone white with afternoon light,
A shadowed dirt road
Curving off who knows where in the distance.
You are leaning against a blue fence,
Legs tan and hair bleached a little from the sun,
My T-shirt tenting your breast.
Years later and a thousand miles removed,
A waiter named Rico lifts his sad eyebrows.
I nod.
I've been drinking at this crummy bar
In the spring dusk of Florida,
Watching the cars go by
With their headlights just on,
Hearing a siren wail.
I don't remember how it was
We came to live in cities,
But I think that somewhere this evening
A man has checked into a cheap motel
And shot himself in the head,
His driver's license and an empty bottle
Laid on the bedside table
For explanation.
Maybe he had a photograph
He couldn't reconcile his life with anymore
And wondered, at the end,
What he had come here hoping to find.
Soon enough now,
I'll be either drunk or out of money,
And there will be nothing to do
But walk back home in the first dark.
I can see on the television
It's cold where you are,

And the sky is failing all across America.
Why were you smiling
That afternoon so long ago?
I can only think we must have been happy.
Somehow that helps.
We are still here, after all,
And it is the same world.

Part Four/ The Green Diamonds of Summer

"On the other side of the left-field wall the agents of death and time
go about the dismal work of the world's corruption. . . . But inside
the park the world is as it was at the beginning. The grass is as
green as it was in everybody's lost childhood; nobody grows old,
and if only the game could last another three innings, or maybe
forever, nobody would ever die."

—Lewis H. Lapham

I

What I love in this isn't what you might think
    If you're my wife Alicia, for example,
Or some stranger driving slowly down our street
    On a Sunday afternoon
In the lush beginnings of the Florida spring,
    Amazed or amused to see a grown man
Throwing, with great seriousness, plastic baseballs
    Repeatedly into the strike zone
Of a welcome mat hung on the fence with clothespins,
    No children in sight.
I could tell you it's something entirely more sublime
    Than the remembered heroes
Or the imagined strikeouts and home runs
    Or even some undying boyhood dream
That keeps me at it far into the first warm afternoons
    Of the year, into the twilight,
Till I can hear Alicia calling me softly from the porch,
    "Lonnie, Lonnie,"

II

As my mother used to call me home for supper
    In Kentucky, long ago.
I can remember the smell of the summer dusk,
    The night birds starting,

The honey-colored horizon fading to blue,
    The field alive with fireflies.
I would always make Dale throw me one more pitch
    After the others had left,
Dale always afraid he'd hit me, saying,
    "I can't even *see* you."
It was like Zen, the ball gone invisible
    In the dark—
Only the sweet buzz of leather and seams on air
    To tell me where it was.
I'd hit it, too, more often than not,

III

    A talent I inherited
From my father, who took me hunting
    In Graves County
Every Thanksgiving and Christmas Day.
    We'd be walking
Tired and numb with cold back to the truck,
    Stars already,
Old Queen inevitably going on point,
    Pap thrashing around
With his boots in the frozen soybean field
    To raise the covey.
And when the quail burst thrumming up, he kneeled
    And lifted his twelve-gauge
Toward what little light there was, the barrel
    Flashing fire.
Then silence, and him half singing to Old Queen,
    "Dead bird there, dead bird . . ."

IV

And him dead now of cancer, who taught me the world
    Not as a man should know it
But as a boy knows it who's outgrown his body
    And gotten good at games.
And I was more than good at baseball,
    Better than Dale,
My best friend even before that first day
    In our backyard
When without meaning to he swung the bat
    Against a clothesline pole,
And the wasps that had built their nest inside it
    Swarmed to cover him.
A week later, when he was well, I sent a line drive
    Into his mother's kitchen.
So we played in the empty field after that.

V

    Year after year
Landscaping a mound and diamond out of the weeds,
    Putting up scraps of chicken wire,
Increasing the distance required for home runs.
    By high school
I'd gotten too strong for the place, driving balls
    Far into the woods.
But we were on the team then, and I just
    Practiced pitching there,
Throwing fastballs through Dale's swing,
    Tying him up with curves,
Letting him hit the ball just often enough
    To keep him from quitting.
"You're gonna throw your arm away," he'd yell,
    And I'd say "Sure," and laugh,
And strike him out again for the twentieth time,

VI

As I struck everybody out
Our senior year with the curveball
They couldn't touch,
Until I let one hang up in the district finals
To a fat first baseman
Who blasted it deep into the blue sky of early summer
For the game's only run.
On the glum bus back to Calvert City,
Dale, seeing me holding
My right elbow, spat Skoal into a Coke can
And smiled:
"Told you you were gonna ruin your arm."
"Fuck you," I said,
Because by this time we were both in love
With Shelley Reynolds,

VII

Who gave not a damn about baseball,
Thus preferring Dale to me,
And not even mildly impressed by our once beating
The hell out of each other over her.
I forgave him, finally, if only because her wishes
Were not to be refused.
The three of us drove to Lake Barkley
Every weekend that summer,
Drinking beer in a dry county, playing the songs
I've forgotten now.
"You like that stuff too much," he'd say
As I opened another Busch,
Knowing it was killing me to watch the two of them.
And Dale married that girl
Who was supposed to live forever,

VIII

But who died in a car
Between Paducah and St. Louis two years later,
    While I was in college in Florida.
I went back for the funeral, and my father's, but not again.
    As Dale had predicted,
I'd thrown my arm away, and I played just well enough
    To keep my scholarship
And learn to make money other ways, marrying
    A girl named Alicia,
Who knows how to handle what money I make
    And knows how to handle me—
For as Dale also predicted, I like the stuff too much.
    I see a few games
During spring training, but mainly chain-smoke
    Through *Monday Night Baseball,*
Finishing cans off just to see how high I can
    Stack them before they fall,

IX

And Alicia appears in her white nightgown,
    Telling me to come to bed.
In my dream of endless extra innings,
    The long drive
That could be the last out failing at the track
    Or the winning homer
Disappearing beautifully over the left-field wall
    Never quite falls,
But rather hangs suspended in the dusk
    Above the field,
Where the lights have just come on
    And swallows glide.
Sometimes I wake up remembering the first ball
    My father gave me, which was plastic;

X

Now it's plastic again, because that's all
    My arm can stand.
But I still have good movement, good control,
    Throwing perfect games out back.
Every year Dale drives down for a visit,
    His face changed
Under that smile of his, and kisses Alicia
    And shakes my hand.
"Lonnie, you bastard," he says when I show him
    The bats and balls
And the welcome mat that serves as a strike zone.
    And, as always,
I strike him out over and over till well past dark,
    When Alicia says, "You boys come in."
And then I make Dale throw me one more pitch,
    Which I usually miss.

THE NEW CITIES
OF THE TROPICS

FOR LAURIE BERRY

It is almost romantic. . . .

—Henry James

Prelude: Late Twentieth-Century Piece

And after pain, the calm—dark records on dark shelves:
Some notion of romance we never got over,
Some sweet past theme we kept trying to recover,
Some concept of ourselves as more than our lost selves.

If we cannot be lovers, we will be players,
Throttling sharp-dressed and muscled, guns in our pockets
For good luck, through the new cities of the tropics—
Deco, palm, flamingo, blues and greens in layers.

This is the dead end of the end of the dead day.
Starlit, remembering what we outlived, we lie
Watching old films of us sweep the ceiling: the sigh
Of flesh on flesh, the cut, and the turning away.

I

Tall Palms

Their loveliness
Is that they seem to need
So little; and their loneliness
That they have only themselves to give back:
Staying out in the dark all night
Where they turn black,
Ordering the blue morning sky,
And looking as if they wished to take flight
On the wind as they thrash and sigh,
Standing still at great speed.

Flamingos

They must have imagined themselves, we think.
Bursting on the montage of *Miami Vice*,
They seem less animal than artifice,
Skinny-legged girls all got up in hot pink.
There is no other gaudiness like theirs.
But to consider one alone is heart-
Breaking. The eye cannot bear them apart.
(Even in plastic, they are sold in pairs.)
And yet they're self-contained as Spanish dancers,
Fully seducing themselves, long necks curled
Into question marks for which no answers
Are required. They know they're here to be seen,
To look good against tropical blue-green.
Unreal, they stride into their unreal world.

Miami

Not the gray, sooty, industrial North
(City you're gone from now for all I know)—
This is the tropics, where Tropical Deco
Blazes stark white in the sun, holding forth
An argument I can hardly fail to follow:
All the sad past comes down to one dear scene
Rich with loss, erotic pink and yellow
Fading to azure and aquamarine.
The sea air smells of rum; the sea is calm.
A cube is missing from the multi-storied
Atlantis condominium, a palm
Dancing sublimely in its place. And tender
Is the night that is falling, memoried
And musical, on this tropical splendor.

Diptych

(Improvisations on a Theme by Jiménez)

1. Mist and Silver: Port Aransas, 1985

In the predawn of an off-season,
The sea swelling with muted moonlight
Along the Gulf Coast of Texas, I couldn't find
The morning star. . . .
                    Shrimp boats
Were just setting out for the day,
So many little lanterns hung with nets,
Sounding their one note:
                    goodbye.

I had my hands stuffed in the pockets
Of a linen jacket the color of gulls;
Invisible gulls were making their first cries
Above the roar of waves washing the rocks
Of the jetty.

            In that off-season,
In that slow shuddering of beginning,
I couldn't find the morning star. . . .
And even then I imagined it was possible
To outlive everything one might have once
Imagined worth living for.

Later, we'd buy shrimp off one of the boats
And take them to our room to boil in beer.
It was still dark, and she was still asleep,
But I was already looking back at the place . . .

—As if from the distant coast of Florida,
                        in the dawn.

91

2. Smoke and Gold: Cedar Key, 1988

When a moon rises to moor the evening star,
The Gulf swells, making the distance to Texas
Irrevocable. . . .
　　　　　　　There are ships out there
That say goodbye repeatedly in your sleep,
Ships that never arrived
Where someone might still stand waiting
On the far shore.

　　　　　　Meanwhile,
There is the magic Floridian hour
When the sea flashes with sunset,
When the sky becomes almost
Tangible in its painterliness, and memory
Rolls loaded dice across the waves. . . .

Still, in the soft metallic resonance of twilight,
The closest thing you have left to a soul
Is the smoke from your cigarette drifting out the window
Of a hotel room, number nine, and what little
You can remember of the little love you made.

And at night here there's nothing to do
But lie down beside your lost self
And the lost selves of others you have lost . . .

—As the dark ghosts of ships
Sound their goodbyes, never arriving
　　　　　　　　　　　　at the far shore.

Tropical Watercolor: Sarasota

Summer sings not far away, and we both know
The errors we've made. The sloped shoulders
Of those palms in the middle distance
Darken; the palms stand solitary as guards.

Summer sings, and against those walls
The late May light has sweetened, the palms
Sigh a little, fronds swaying in the breeze,
Making a sad watercolor of the square.

A mackerel sky frames the square, the square
We dreamed failed us in this place we'd come to
To find ourselves again as in a mirror.
Love, this is the square that failed.

I broke myself trying to make myself strong
For you. Dusk gilds white buildings, and smoke
From my cigarette floats toward the stars
That aren't there yet, the stars we used to desire.

They are a vast absence, reminding me
I don't believe in anything anymore except
The difficulty of everything for men and women.
Your remembered ghost is the ghost of my grandmother

Walking here endlessly in a black dress,
Shadow lost among the shadows of palms
On this square that failed, blocks from the sea.
I have run out of life, for what?

I have run out of life from the repetition
Of our moving only from mirror to mirror,
Catching our reflections in shop windows
And finding them less real than mannequins.

Tropical Lament

It rains so long and hard here, I'm remembering
All the rain of my childhood, the pearls
Of hail I'd hold in my hands
After a storm.

This rain isn't going to stop
Until it's made a moat around me,
A grave the shape of a ring.
                              This rain
Is falling now wherever she is, who survives me;
It's soaking her clothes through to the skin,
Which used to be all fire.

When will it finally drown me?
Sometimes, remembering her hips, I feel afraid.
Sometimes I'm afraid she's gone—
That memory and music are all that's left of her.

But I'm tired of the rain's dark harmony.
I'm tired of everybody telling me:
Lift yourself up, never go down!
Don't we maybe lift ourselves, going down?

And the rain keeps singing on this coast without a sea.

Tropical Deco

(Miami Beach)

The sea deepened at dusk between yacht masts,
And through the summer nights the seawind blew
Across the balconies and terraces
Of lost hotels with lost names like the Sands,

Their friezes carved with figures, ampersands,
Flowers, shells, flamingos, rich surfaces
The sun bleached all day long, till powder blue,
Pink, and seafoam green fell away like masks,

Leaving the blocks of stone white as the sands
Where women strolled with pale, composed faces
Under parasols, performers in a masque
Long since ended, frozen into tableau,

Faded into a past memory erases
Of all but romance, the aroma of musk,
And the faint strains of some tropical blues
Or jazz—lament for the well-dressed thousands

At Hialeah, amassed in the stands,
Loving the taboo, losing the races.

Florida Twilight, 1905

(St. Augustine)

Returning late, the flushed West to the right,
One saw, aligned against the golden sky
(The very throne-robe of the star-crowned night),
Black palms, a frieze of chiseled ebony.
And even at the moment one resolved
Not to come back, the scent of fruit and flowers
Brought on a sadness as the past dissolved:
Arcades, courts, arches, fountains, lordly towers. . . .

The shore of sunset and the palms, meanwhile—
Late shade giving over to greater shade—
What were they? With what did they have to do?
It was like a myriad pictures of the Nile,
But with a History yet to be made,
A world already lost that was still new.

II

Daisy Miller in the Colosseum

One-half of the gigantic circus was in deep shade,
The other was sleeping in the luminous dusk. . . .
And here, perhaps, the author pauses to ask
Himself the force of the fine distinctions made
Between mere "intimacy" and "lawless passion"—
Whether they are in fact more consequential
Than the harder architecture of the action:
The present "historic atmosphere," or the castle
At Vevay. For this is, too, a story
Of the body, its beauty, and the desire
That undoes it one evening in the glory
Of dark archways, the moonlit miasma of Rome . . .
And still there was something American in the gyre
Of the moon, though the moon was far from home.

Aphrodite Holding a Seashell

It isn't only that she has no arms
Anymore, or that the shoulders slope down
From no face over the breasts to a chasm
Like a Caesarean scar, or that the gown
Can hardly keep its hold on those white hips,
Or even that there's no trace of the fingertips
That once touched the shell's fluted opening—
The loss was always implicit as the longing.
Still, we like to believe it's only desire
That keeps the shell there where her sex should be:
The stone making soft waves, a marble flower,
Holding not the sound of the sea but only
The frail ghost of that sound, a memory,
Like a bell in some abandoned tower.

Fin de Siècle

In the twilight of the nineteenth century,
    Chekhov's peasants
Are gazing across the river and dreaming
    The afterlife begins
In the belfry of the church with five domes.
    In Moscow one longs
For the provinces, and in the provinces
    One longs for Moscow.
This is the desire that makes life at once
    Irresistible and unbearable.
A man takes his lover's soft shoulders in his hands,
    Her hair gone suddenly gray.
In the chiaroscuro of the first snows of autumn,
    In the boom and heave
Of ice breaking up on the river in spring, you hear
    Your life passing like a song.
Near Petersburg, the women go mad trying to keep
    The geese out of the garden.

Sherwood Anderson, 1912

To his secretary, with that American laugh
        That can mean anything:
"I have been wading in a long river
        And my feet are wet."
And so disappears into a world suspended
        Between Thanksgiving
And the new fiscal year, walking eastward
        Along a railroad track
Somewhere between Elyria and Cleveland,
        Five or six dollars
In his pocket, a pint of whiskey. The day
        Is like a silent movie
Based on a slow-moving chapter in a bad novel.
        He has, in fact,
Been wading in a river, a nearly bare maple
        Hugging its bank.
He is writing fragments on scraps of paper,
        Imagining winged seeds
Whirling crazily about, filling the air.
        In the serene milk
Of the sky, everything's properly punctuated,
        Nothing's misspelled.
Above the maple, stark against the sky—
        Crossties and a bridge,
Beyond which a new life might begin. . . .
        But this is
The terrible mythology of the real:
        A nameless boy's head
Smashed against a brick wall in a Cleveland alley,
        While in an office in Chicago
A man goes mad staring into the black space
        Around a column in a ledger.
Now, in the early winter dusk of Ohio,
        The trees are tall dark girls

Left out in the cold. He makes a small fire,
　　Pulls the pint of whiskey
From his coat, and says to no one but water,
　　"Let me tell you a story."
Ink that was words blurs on the scraps of paper
　　Floating off down the river,
Just as a last maple leaf the color of fire
　　Trembles and drifts away—
Beyond the scope of anybody's loneliness
　　Or anybody's desire.

Elegy for Roland Barthes

"I don't think he needs an elegy."

—my ex-wife

They do not need us,
Any more than last year's leaves
Are signs of anything
Unless we make them so for our sake,
As I am doing now.
Here on the back porch,
In the twilight,
It is merely spring,
And the leaves that fell or the wind shook loose
Make one darkness
With the season's first green shoots.
But the white gown you have hung from the line
Shines. Phosphorescent,
It catches what light the sky can manage yet
And moves, and is alive.
And if it is only wind,
Say that the wind, for our sake,
Needs a form,
And that your white gown
Lifting there in the dark
Makes a possibility of wind and darkness,
While the language of children
Fades along the street.
I cannot remember
When spring seemed less than a miracle,
When my body made any pretense it would last,
When summer began like anything
But a memory of summer.
There is something beautiful
About what returns inevitably,
Though what is gone
Is perhaps also beautiful

By its own code,
But which we translate:
Later—the street silent, no wind;
A white gown shining in starlight
For no one.

III

Little Testament

Whatever the night is,
I'd tell you it's the heaving mass
Inside somebody's kicked skull,
A dark so dark that intricate things begin to shine
Like a snail's trail,
Like the lights strung out like cheap beads
Along some city street
Where people work and dream and die.
I don't say live.
                        From a distance,
The city looks like broken glass
You see in any city lot
Under the faint, faithless chant
Of streetlamps.
                        South of the city, too,
The Spanish chapel is without faith—
Is merely sad and lovely as the flowered dress
Of the girl who sweeps the chapel steps at dawn,
Or as the girl herself whose eyes
Won't meet your eyes, or as the dust
That seems to resurrect itself
Wherever she's just swept.

You can already tell I have nothing
To offer you beyond this flash of hope, this echo
Fading as it ranges westward
Across a continent that can, at night,
Still seem nearly empty.
                        Mine is the one
Window left lit as you walk
Through this neighborhood and through this night

That quicken your step.
                    And the night
Keeps coming back, as if you were the one
Returning to it—moments
When you hear what sounds like hell's orchestra
Blasting from a car,
Or when what you're afraid of seems to drift
Close to the shore of whatever river
You love:
                  Ohio, Mississippi, Rio Grande.

When now fails,
Was is all there is;
Elsewhere we lose always.
My cigarette smoke floating off in the night
Is the fire of my autobiography in ashes.

We only win at trying not
To be.
           But anybody
Can tell you that—can call
Escape pride,
Meanness humility,
The arc and hiss of a match flicked into the water
The deep brief love they once felt for the world.

What little they find in my pockets
When it's over,
                you can have.

The Lights at Newport Beach

If there were time for everything
(And there is); if that phosphorescent light
Stunning the Pacific meant anything
(And it does); if all this world of worlds might
Become more than the museum for something
We have lost (and it will) . . . but not tonight.
Tonight, love, Newport Beach is simply on fire,
The buildings blazing up under the sky,
The streets running headlong into the sea.
If we were more than the sum of our desire
(But we're not); if there were a language I
Could find to get beyond the opacity
Of zero. . . . But I'm tired of words and all we turn
Away from. I just want to watch it burn.

Laguna Beach Breakdown

You had come searching for a second chance,
But trying to break through, merely broke down,
Until at last any sense of purpose
Seemed nothing more than something else to lose.
You let it go and, seeing no reason to mourn
What you could no longer name, kept silence
Under the vast vacuum of a heaven
Someone had nailed stars up to to hold in place.
You were hoping maybe a change of season
Might help, but there was none. You woke at dawn
Shuddering in the indifferent embrace
Of your own arms, unable to turn or return,
Dreaming of drowning, neutral as seaweed in the war
The sea continually waged against the shore.

Sardis Reservoir, Mississippi

A place of memory: the beach at evening,
Windswept, and the lake spreading out into darkness.
The wind makes small waves on the water,
And the waves, catching moonlight, kiss the sand.

But the three boys drinking beer on the beach
Don't have any memories yet. It isn't
Quite summer, and they're not quite men.
They talk about girls, each of them lying.

They rode out here with some friends,
And the friends drove off and left them.
They've been wading in the cold water,
Their pants wet to the thighs, shoes full of sand.

Every few minutes or so a car goes by
On the road above the beach, headlights
Sweeping the sand. It's miles back to town.
If they can't catch a ride, they'll have to walk.

The boys are drunk and wish they had more beer.
The wind off the water is cold as they start to walk,
Talking about what they'd do if they had a girl.
They don't realize they've gotten what they came for.

The memories already forming themselves
Were like those moonlit waves on the lake, breaking.

In Pieces

Outside, the crickets syncopate as if
Searching for each other. The streetlight lends
A mellow golden cast to everything,
And the shouts of young people fade away
In the rumblings of engines, which also
Fade away.

      And stationed by this window,
I know I won't sleep again tonight.
I've done this long enough now to believe
That if I turn away, all will be lost.

Movies in pieces running through my head
Don't help. The stars don't help—they aren't there
Tonight. And if I drove, where would I drive?
From the beginning I was both necessary
And beside the point, the kid always
The kid, whom you'd overlook completely,
Did he not break your heart.

         Somewhere not more
Than a block from here, a woman writhing in the sweat
Of her body tries to dream herself out.
What morning forgives, the night will not let go.
The story never changes, never ends.

And what's left us in pieces all these years
Continues. We've come to love it the way
The tortured, in the religion of their pain,
Become their own tormentors and start to think:

How could it be otherwise?

In Memory of the Boys of Dexter, Kentucky

West of Murray, just off 641,
It is forever summer in my mind.
I see land darken under a red sun
And hear lost music drift back on the wind.
Blind fingers read the initials *D.P.*
Carved in the oak from which he was found hung;
In the creek, *J.* holds his breath endlessly.
Did they think they were late, leaving so young?—
Chain-smoking only to bypass cancer,
Washing down pills with whiskey, wrapping cars
Round poles like a girl's love ring. . . . In answer,
The sky fades like a chord behind first stars.
Their dying, it seems now, started at birth—
Dying to find out what their lives were worth.

Meditation at Kentucky Dam

I'd say the sky still pink as a fading love-
Bite in the west is draining into the lake
On the other side of the dam—I'd
Say that, if I didn't know better.

These sultry summers spent brooding
In a Southern resort town get harder
The older I get, and the slim brown girls
Migrating from Michigan and Wisconsin,
Though they still allure me, have become
Untouchable now.
                                    I like
To watch them tying their hair back,
Padding along the floodwall as if they'd grown
Beautiful stilts and mastered them.

The lights across the river move
On the moving water like a pencil sketch.
                            This river empties
Into the Ohio just northeast of Paducah,
And you can finish the story from there.

I've tried and tried to reject old music,
To admit no cognizance of the depths,
But tonight the last light falls in such a way
As to probe the water and illume the shadow-
Shapes of nameless things.

                        Lost one:
I sometimes believe your chill blood
Fills my hands: I cannot move them.
The stars and a meager piece of moon begin
To swim, as though seen from underwater.

Still, I'll walk back to my car and drive away.

I'd have to drag the river to find you now.

The Mississippi at Barfield, Arkansas

Sitting poised on the sinister shore,
We pass a fifth of bourbon back and forth
And flick spent Marlboros hissing into the water.
It's midsummer. The huge barge headed north

Hardly moves at all, and the Southern dusk,
From here, doesn't so much come as go—
A conflagration in the trees behind us,
But a dying of our sky, sordid and slow.

The river looks as if it's praying for rain;
Boys in loud cars are praying for the twelfth
Time tonight to drown or get laid. Mark Twain
Is dead, and I don't feel too well myself.

There's nothing I'd like better than to rescue you
From Arkansas, where you're the loveliest thing
I know this side of the levee, my blue-
Bonnet, black-eyed Susan the drought is killing.

On the far shore, in the afterlife of Tennessee,
Some cattle have wandered down to the sand to drink.
But there's no way across there for you and me,
No bridge nearer than Memphis—and I don't think

That if we tried to swim we'd stand a chance.
It's dark. I'm wondering how long my liver
And lungs can keep me with you, wanting just once
To wind up on the right side of the river.

The Parthenon at Nashville

Late December noon, near freezing—
Maple and sweetgum bare, but the grass green yet
In sunlight, and warmth of light wearing away
At the frail scythe's-edge of ice
Around the pond. On her lunch hour,
Parked in his car, they tossed the last
Of their sandwiches to ducks that bobbed and fussed
In the smaller oval of water not frozen over.
They were beyond being
In love, but not quite ready
To look past the end of the affair.
Across the water, reflected in the water,
Risen stone:
Columns swelling with light,
The stylized figures restored
To the frieze—an order
Called into question
By the troubled surface of the pond.
They remember wondering
What happened to the ducks
Come autumn. Now they know: nothing.
And now a solitary jogger pushes his breath
Past them, as the traffic continues
Out on West End.
They sense that something
Needs to be done or said—
Anything but this feeling of themselves
As figures held in the motion
Of some lost moment.
And yet they can't seem to move, to speak,
Maybe thinking they won't have this clarity
Again for a long time, maybe amazed
At the distance from which they see themselves:
Luminous, hardly human,
And already half in love with the beautiful ruins.

IV

The Summer Elegies

Aubade

Somehow they're never quite what we meant them to be,
 Our lives and the little music
  We make of them.
These early darknesses we rise to could be
 Anywhere—could be the same place
  Or a thousand miles apart.

Even as I was waking today, I dreamed we were
 Driving along the Gulf Coast again,
  High summer
And the cities with beautiful names slipping past:
 Pensacola, Mobile, Pascagoula,
  New Orleans.

In that ripe twilight, water and sky were one
 Luminous blue, a landward breeze
  Dying under the dark
Of cypresses draped with Spanish moss.
 We couldn't stay, any more
  Than the light could,

And this morning, watching the sky bleed pale mauve,
 I saw the dense, vegetal wall of Florida
  Fill the window,
And thought of you, still sleeping in a Houston predawn,
 Bringing the night's last dream to a close.
  It is the old story,

But the old story suffices when it's all there is:
 Birds starting and the first light

Coming on—
Coming on like a minor chord struck and held,
Shaping something out of the silence
Even as it fades away.

The Beginning of Summer

Rain most afternoons now, and the azaleas
    Over already—
A pink and lavender wreckage on the lawn
    Like the aftermath
Of some grand celebration. The petals
    Echo obscenely
Our pair of plastic pink flamingos
    Held still on stilts
Beside the birdbath, under the eaten cedar,
    While new arrivals
Busy the feeder and thrash in the water:
    Tufted titmouse,
Cardinal, jay, woodpecker, mourning dove.
    They seem ghosted
As you are sometimes by the memory of Jane,
    The dead white cat.
First sunset, then twilight, and now a few stars
    Adrift in the pines.
All that can returns, as it must, for no reason
    Except desire.

Hurricane

I dreamed of nothing; I would rise at dawn.
And you'd still be asleep when I got back,
The air conditioner humming against the hundred-
Degree Houston noon. That summer, even now,
Is a haze of silence, a haze of sweat,
Interminable afternoons when, lost in my long
Alcohol, I'd wait for the sun to burst
In the high window facing west, sometimes
A bluebird fussing on a black, dead branch.
And yet the plum trees flowered through the heat,
Putting out livid petals, and the palm
Sat squat and stolid across the street, dry fronds
Lifting a little, then subsiding. I'd stand
Under the skylight in the Rothko Chapel
And feel nothing at all, those huge
Late canvases like panes smeared dark with blood.
If there was any holiness, it was
The thrill resembling madness that I felt
Making the change from 59 to I-45
In heavy traffic, downtown towering
So near the overpass it seemed as if
I could leap there. Later, too tired to sleep
Without whiskey and pills, I'd lie awake
With a towel over my eyes, touching
The soft backs of your legs below your panties.
And when I couldn't touch you, couldn't respond
To even the simplest of questions, it wasn't
Any reflection on the desire I felt
For you, though it must have appeared that way.
If anything, it was a profusion of desire,
A longing so inarticulate I almost
Broke down once in the Safeway, watching
A plain-faced housewife pushing a cart
Past rows of fruit. It's humorous, but true.
And what I remember seeing under the towel,

Eyes closed and waiting for the chemicals
To darken my blood, was how unreal the sky
Had looked that day just before the hurricane
Finally broke, and the hard rains began.
When it was over, the sun exploded
Through the dripping trees, and we walked the block,
A slaughter of pearls decorating each lawn.

August Elegy

You write that you are tired,
That even language has failed you,
That each sentence doubts itself halfway through.
I start to type, "This rage
For order . . ." but run out of words,
And the letters fall to pieces on the page.

Monday arrives wordless,
Sun-struck, August wind in the chimes
As birds flit past, elusive as their names.
Last week a black guy bigger
Than me, and much to my surprise,
Pronounced me to be an "artificial nigger."

Otherwise, there's no sound
Of anyone else's voice for days
On end, save yours through the splice and fray
Long distance. I watch, I
Wait for the mail to come around,
Then stand there disappointed under the sky.

This living alone is
Endless language left unmeasured,
And the slow coming on of sleep a pleasure
Sadder than being young.
I wake to speak, and the word *was*
Breaks sweeter than any berry on my tongue.

Wild Horses

When you can't get beyond the wall we've built,
    They take you there.
I've seen your eyelids fluttering in sleep,
    Dreams of green fields
Flecked with dew and the sun just coming up
    As you ride out
Of yourself and into a Florida
    Lost before you
Arrived, before there was the dirt oval
    Outside Ocala
With its few wild palms, and even before
    The land was named,
When wild horses ran that are bones of stone.
    But you love, too,
The names: Reckless Passion, Lady of Spain. . . .
    Hialeah,
You told me, sounds like bright silks, money gone,
    A soft dawn sky.
They take you there, your hair dark as the mane
    You hold onto.

Elegy at Summer's End

Now the darker cloth is drawn from closets,
The summer dresses put away
Whose flowers fade faster than even summer's own.
Now a minor music begins:
First frost and newfound clarity of sky.

I've left you sleeping in the summerhouse
To walk the loved edge of the lake
Where the southward flight of geese is more heard than seen,
As this summer may come to seem
A season less remembered than invented.

Already there have been too many words,
Too many versions of the way
The light fell across the water some certain dusk
And the "stunned" trees on the far shore
Caught fire: *candescence, conflagration, blaze.*

Now the darker cloth is drawn from closets,
And we who loved the world must learn
The language of absence: days foreshortened, empty rooms,
The irrevocable distance
Between the goodbye and the letting go.

ADULT SITUATIONS

TO JON ANDERSON

&

FOR REBECCA BYRKIT

"And it seemed to them that in a little while the solution would be found, and that then a new, beautiful life would begin. And they both realized that the end was still far off, and that the hardest, the most complicated part was only just beginning."

—Chekhov, "The Lady with the Dog"

One

The Circumstances

If strength is love, then we weren't strong enough,
But if strength is letting love go, we were.
Men among men, we couldn't trust each other.
With women, it was ourselves we couldn't trust.

It had to do with houses and with cars,
With what had to be done and with money.
We wound up loving money like a country
In a country we loved like women, its stars

Transposed from flag to night sky, its lithe palms
Lonely beyond all hope of consolation.
Night after night, the festive repetition
Of food and drink, of music and new films . . .

—It failed us, finally, or else we failed it.
We never brought the long quarrel with our fathers
To a close, and so never saw our daughters
Until they'd drifted away like money spent.

It rained then. And suddenly the faces
Of our wives were older, our faces were old,
The screens went blank, the light dimmed, and the cold
Came to stay for good in our white houses.

Dying, what we remembered of our lives
Was nothing more or less than simply talking
About nothing in particular, walking
Nowhere down dark streets with other men's wives.

Death in Orange County

It's in the way the waves fall like dull lead,
Water warmer by September but still cold,
The bougainvillea's crinoline, fresh blood,

The sky's blank face, the blank face of a child.
A skywriter spells SURRENDER. To what?
This ease? This difficulty? Of the mild

Astonishments of a Saturday night,
Not one survives—not her face, not her name,
Not her. And certainly not how the light

Spilled broken on the bay and made a game
Of whatever it was you were trying
To make clear between you there, over rum.

Sometimes you don't feel like doing anything.
Sometimes you're done before you even rise.
It's in the way the sun mutes everything,

The mist, the fog, the high latticed fences.
The girl on the plane was reading a book:
Death of a "Jewish American Princess."

Sometimes you don't know quite what you feel like.
You put on your favorite disc, *Camelot,*
And walk around the house having the look.

A good part of the time, you feel like shit.
It's in the stylishness of restaurants,
In the sweet note of a single gunshot

Echoing off the glass of lit storefronts,
In the cool distances of these houses.
Nobody knows what anybody wants,

Or else knows all too well what those tan faces
Are trying hard not to show they don't feel.
And all that's left to you now are traces:

House, stock, Jacuzzi, clothes, automobile.

Ballroom Dancing in the Barrio

South Tucson wind would blow away the stars
If they weren't nailed in place above the night
As we arrive in loud clothes and loud cars
That slink like dealers in the parking lot
Where bulldozers muscle up to mangle
What's left of the barrio. Here, a girl
Could lose it all in one serpentine tango,
In the Scotch-cigarette-and-salsa swirl
Of this lit synergy, this dying to live—
Heat of black silk on flesh, a slow burning
In the slick bilinguistics of desire.
Coming to get what we can't come to give,
We shine and shine on, querulous, turning.
We weren't just dancing, see. We were on fire.

Metropolitan Twilight

Mid-May: day warm but cooling down
As afternoon ripens past ripeness
And shadows increase their claim.
Through any window you happen
To look out of, the world is
Lush with the contrived imagery
Of shrub and thick grass, pine and palm,
While beyond it all the blue
Of the bare sky goes deep
With anticipation of stars.

Down the block, the last lawnmower
Chortles out, and children disappear
Into the sound of their own shouts.
A woman shakes out a sheet
And drapes it over a cord
Where it billows alive in breeze.
Otherwise the scene is ghostless,
Or ghosted only with a promise
Having nothing to do with the past.
For there's no place here for the past—

Not with winter seeming so far away,
And summer heavy in the held breath
Of the world's various green,
And the huge planes passing over
Now, and now, and the passengers
Beginning to undo their seatbelts
And order cocktails, their thoughts
Most surely hundreds of miles
Ahead of them: of summer,
Of lovers in other cities.

And there's no telling what might
Be happening now behind the sun-

Struck windows of the eight-story
Apartment building up the street,
Nor in the topmost towerings
Of skyscrapers downtown,
The southwest sides of which
The late light has, touching, turned
To gold. Watching, you wouldn't have
Thought it possible that the world

Could go on transforming this way
Its already perfected self,
Or that the moment, turned inward, might
Yield such inklings of the eternal.
And it is like this. And it is
Like this till, of a sudden,
Sky's blue and world's green meld
In marine light, and all along
The avenues the streetlamps
Flicker on, making incandescent

Globes of silver for moths
To flutter through, and in the un-
Prepared-for return to the self,
You are sad for you couldn't say
What reason. And in this in-
Between time and in-between season,
The heart cries out for what it dreams
It has lost. It is the hour
When a man might decide to rise
And walk to the corner store

For an evening newspaper,
But stops on the sidewalk and turns.
He sees the house he's lived in all
These years and, through the window,
His wife reading in lamplight,
And wonders, perhaps, how his life
Came to happen to him this way,

And what it's meant, and how much
Longer it will be before his body
Fails, or his wife's body fails,

And the dream they both always knew
The ending of comes finally true.
And turns again, and walks, hands
Clutching the familiar contents
Of his pockets. He sees one jet
Winking westward, the first star
Pulsing on. And through the tangled
Fingers of some trees, the moon, for him,
Is a bright, magnificent coin
That can't be spent in this world.

South Boulevard

In the unfamiliar silence,
In the slow, intensive dusk
    Of a Houston July,
It was as if the trees, arcing
To entangle, made a vaulted nave
    Of the street.

Cicadas were starting to sing
In the leaf-green half-light
    As, here and there,
A porch light stuttered on,
And the first soft chords of evening
    Struck the houses.

Strangers to that good neighborhood,
The two of you were simply
    Strolling through,
Anxious to begin what you could not
Have known would be a future filled
    With absence.

There is a certain distance
At which the image of someone
    You once loved
Takes form and grows beautiful,
And a certain distance at which
    It disappears,

Lost in the particular light
Of a summer's evening,
    On that street
Above which the limbs of live oaks
Interlocked delicately as the fingers
    Of folded hands.

Near

San Francisco

1

Again this sense of something almost over,
    Something about to begin—
All too often a matter of mood, pragmatics.
    In the city,
In the first afternoon chill announcing
    The end of summer,

You watched women blowing past in pressed skirts,
    Their faces distant, pale,
The lights just starting to come on high up
    In the buildings,
A workman with a jackhammer singing
    "If I Had a Hammer."

2

In the city, you had a momentary vision
    Of pamphlets raining down
From the deep blue sky, the good propaganda,
    Irrefutable.
And, in the city, you wondered what all the small
    Catastrophes that compose

The gone summers of our biographies
    Might finally add up to,
If you could add them up. It was almost
    September, almost dark,
And you had no place in particular
    To be.

Soon

Soon, these great stadiums will be empty,
Standing coolly at twilight, lit only
By the twilight, and there will be no sound,
No echo and no memory of sound.

Soon, these mansions along North Boulevard
Will fall into disrepair, then will fall,
Their foundations given over to grass
Under the vaulted naves of the live oaks.

These freeways won't dream of rush-hour traffic.
These towers won't give you the time of day.
These storefronts won't show the season's fashion.
Nobody will try to take your money.

Soon, no one will remember how it was
To drive home at the end of the long day,
To hear a song you thought you'd forgotten,
To sleep and rise and not know quite what for.

And no one will remember what it was
To try to live and love and make love live
In these times we belong to but call ours,
Near the end of what looked like forever.

Dawn

Washington, D.C.
January 1, 1990

Pigeons sail through the rivers and canyons
Of darkness between buildings. Now their wings
Burnish in the new light above rooftops.

Above rooftops, smoke bruised purple by the cold
Clots in the sky. In the sky, the first jet
Pulses its signal westward, disappears.

Cabs glide past the sleepless in their black coats.
And in two tall hotels across a square,
Two people exchange gazes from the lit frames

Of their rooms—anonymous silhouettes,
Almost without gender from this distance,
But with everything in the world in common.

Two

The Dead Gods

It is no longer clear where we're going.
There is no longer light along the road,
Dark roads. The roads go dark outside Dallas
And darken outside Washington, D.C.
It seems there's nothing left to do but sing,
But sing what? Whatever little we had
In us of music has gone out of us,
Lost on some dark road outside some city.

If they come back now, it's only to die
Again, far less beautifully than we'd care
To imagine to remember. Now shelves
Heavy with all we loved fall down, the sky
Is full of static, dusk soars, and the air
Is lovely with us who have just ourselves.

Kennedy, King, Lennon, etc.

The New Gods

And then, for a long time, nothing happened.
The citizens slept in the sleeping cities
And rose at dawn and worked and loved and slept.
Nobody knew just how long this would last.

It happened because it wanted to happen.
Young, sculptural, the gods rose in the cities.
Lush, sexual, they shone as the citizens slept.
Lovely, they filled the screens but couldn't last.

It happened because it had to happen.
Moving sleepless through the sleepless cities,
Filling the dreams of citizens who slept,
They too just wanted to sleep at the last.

Not from the snow-marbled heights of mountains,
Not from the deep blue rivers the snow made,
Not from the sweet blue nowhere of the sky,

But from the scented gloss of magazines,
From New York, Houston, and L.A., they came—
To become immortal, and then to die.

Woodshedding: Kentucky, 1980

The Seventies glittered faintly behind us—
Untouchable cities, distant as stars;
Punk and New Wave arrived only in rumors.
And still the blue winter dusk would find us
Assembled, armed with loud amps, cheap guitars,
Hands ready to bleed for as many hours
As it took to hear something nearly ours
Among the bold clichés: girls, death, and cars.
The notebook turned yellow, naive pages
Heavy with the desire to be anywhere
But those small-town basements and garages
That swelled like hammered thumbs—places haunted
Now with whatever it was we left there
To find whatever it was we wanted.

Lines for Hank Williams

The way his high voice would break and break down,
Beautifully lonesome, lost . . . who once wrote
A song at gunpoint in a hotel downtown,
Fingers shaking to hold the simple chords.
The world was one long night, endless Nashvilles,
A jambalaya of women, whiskey, and pills.
At the Opry they poured coffee down his throat
Backstage before the show, until he'd cough
And rise, trying to remember his own words.
And once, driving through the dark of the night
In a Cadillac with Minnie Pearl, he broke
Into "I Saw the Light," then broke it off,
His voice losing volume as he spoke:
"There ain't no light, Minnie. There ain't no light."

Stanzas on the Anniversary of Hart Crane's Death

Gainesville, Florida
April 27, 1988

Evening now, and sunlight burnishing
The bleached white slabs of apartment buildings.
Girls glide by coolly on the street. Tall palms

Sway a little in a little wind
As, tremulous, the day begins to fail,
Then finds itself again, flared by neon.

The thump of rubber against the concrete
Raquetball courts has perhaps something to say
About sadness, repetition, romance . . .

—Or perhaps not, any more than the green fins
Of the palmetto, with a last shot of light
Behind them, resemble gold wings, wedges

Of lime lipping bottles of Corona.
And yet there is something inexplicably sad
About the way squeezed lime clouds golden beer,

Some pulsing rhythm among the soft globes
Of the streetlamps, and something hopelessly
Romantic in the way the points of palms

Aspire to a sky already fading.
(It is only the legend of your youth
Lost to all the real things you learned to love.)

Fifty miles away, the Gulf of Mexico
Teases the nostrils, rousing a desire
Bacardi and cigarettes cannot cure,

And which no well-intentioned lover
Can fulfill wholly or for long. It is
Always yourself again, left all alone

At evening's end, strolling down the same street
You knew the dead end to by heart in childhood,
But somehow lovelier than you remembered . . .

—Especially at this late hour when, to the west,
The twilight plays the game it loves to lose
And loses, over and over, to its dark sea.

West Kentucky Quintet

I. Then

Then, everything sang.
Then, the girl whose pants I undid, breathless,
As she, breathless, undid mine,
Smelled of honeysuckle, clean flesh.
Then I lost her face among the faces of leaves
In a stand of poplars.

Then, I ran and ran.
Then, the porchlights floated across an empty field,
The stars just coming on at dusk
And the dusk just coming on.
Then, the night, claiming everything, claimed everything,
And I rose to sleep.

Then, it rained and rained.
Then, the summer deepened too far to remain summer,
Everything too green for its own good,
The first leaves turning, then falling.
And then the long rain was beginning to end,
And then it wasn't.

II. Back Then

The boys of Dexter
Don't come around anymore.
They've crashed their cars out on old 641,
Drowned drunk in Calloway Creek,
Or slunk off at dusk

Into the bottoms
With illiterate local girls
Who giggle, ovulating, anxious to marry.

They haven't been seen since
And won't again.

Show me the best
Of the little of what's left.
I want to get one last look at all this
And try hard to remember
What it took me years

To forget so much of.
Tell me again how it was
Back then—how the train used to stop at the store.
Point out the vine-choked foul poles
In the baseball field

Given over to milo.
Let's tear it up this one last time
And run that Chrysler ragged past midnight
Down those dark and dangerous roads
We drove in our sleep.

Tell me about the girls
Back then, and I'll tell you
About the cool, sleek women in the big cities.
All the hell romance is, after all,
Is what you don't got.

III. Back

The sun has just slunk down into the Ohio River,
But the huge catfish skulking at the base
Of Kentucky Dam don't know it.

Over the lit-up dusk and noise of the Paducah Raceway,
Three geese are beating hell southward
In the sky's cold blood.

Somehow, every time I'm gone I'm gone long enough
    To forget with what intensity
        I hate this place.

In Sandy's I smoke a pack and a half and drink longneck Buds,
    Pronouncing "thing" "thaing" to the sweet dumb smile
        Of the girl behind the bar.

Later a good ole boy kindly offers up the information
    That the woman I've danced every slow song with
        The last set is a "psychobitch."

I can remember moments in summer when this country was
    beautiful
    To me, but tonight in the white of the moon
        See only satellite dishes.

If you can get past the ignorance and indolence,
    The racism and sexism, the people
        Are good enough people—

But dying, and dying with brutal regularity,
    Of gunshot wounds, car wrecks,
        And lung cancer.

IV. Hell and Back

I nearly died once in Oxford, Mississippi,
And nearly died in Houston.
The water's gunmetal tonight in Kentucky
Under the pittance of a moon.

If you who died here
Have been dead long enough, maybe you could tell me
Whether the water down there's strong enough
To get as drunk on as we used to like to be.

—Not that talk's forgiveness, never that.
There's been too many changes, too little change.
But you know how lonely it can get
Here by Johnathan Creek Bridge.

For what it's worth, I lost the woman
I fought you for trying to take. I hear
No sound of a voice, nobody swimming,
But that's all right. I understand. Stay there.

V. Hell

In the only photograph
I had of you, you were lying
Passed out on the hood of a '76 Cutlass
Parked in the yard in front of your trailer.
I was lying face-down in wet grass.
We'd been drinking gin all day
And smoking pot.

Your wife,
As I recall, took the picture
For a joke. Your wife, as I recall,
Was not lovely, arranged magnets
In animal shapes on the refrigerator
For your three kids, smoked four packs

Of Marlboros a day, and once
Came on to me in the kitchen

With you in the next room.
And you, as I recall,
Weren't terribly bright,
Were always smiling,
And would do almost any fool thing
For anybody.

                    In the photograph
        The summer night is coming down

        Over the trailer park,
        Our bodies white, the red road
        Turning white in the distance—
        Years before your wife left,
        Before you got laid off,
        Before the power company
        Cut the lights in the trailer.

        And one evening you wired the door shut
        And swallowed a bottle of Seconal
        And lay down in the dark.
        You signed the note asking everyone
        And God to forgive you "Love."
        Lord knows what
        Became of the photograph.

Insurance Men at Breakfast:
Lexington, Kentucky, 1969

Black ties, black coffee, cigarettes, cigars,
And talk of what the trouble these days is
That forces them to mortgage the duplexes
They'll have to mortgage again in a few years.
They love this hour away from what they love,
This quiet before the day begins its grind,
This talk of work, of baseball, and beyond:
"Any word on your boy over there, Steve?"

A silence, then somebody tells some joke
About a hippie or a black,
About a salesman whose new blond, Frances,
Ran off to Louisville and won't be back.
So much smoke floats up around their faces,
It's hard to see their faces for the smoke.

American Tragedy

The Chevrolet fires past two blond children
Eating mud in the ditch by a dirt road.
Kentucky, midsummer, sun going down—
Day like an empty shotgun shell, still warm,
Fragrant with dog shit and honeysuckle.

The skinny girl inside the white trailer
Is drinking gin and torturing herself
With a cigarette: nipples, navel, crotch.
The screen door hangs by one broken finger.
Past dark, a light comes on. Nothing happens.

Watching Bergman Films with My Father

What you can't quite appreciate
In angles, lighting, and camera work,
You make up for
With your deep understanding of despair,
The gray that flickers in the dark
And fingers your gray face.

It's nothing new to you, really,
This sense of loss at things falling away,
Life in shadow.
You've felt everything that you're feeling now
And lived these scenes in your own way,
Only less artfully.

And so you're not surprised that the girl
Goes mad in God's absence, or that the man
Just shoots himself
By the river, or that the smoke and filth
Choking the lungs of a woman
Almost isn't painful

Seen from this distance. We don't talk
About it or talk about anything.
Outside, the sky
Is preparing to darken and to die
Without color, stars. Everything
Is ready for the walk

We'll take because there's nothing else
To do, because we need the world, if it
Doesn't need us.
Despite our differences, there isn't much
Difference between us tonight,
And there's nobody else.

Alcohol

Waking late, I hit REDIAL on the phone
    To maybe hear the voice
Of whoever it was I talked with last—

Whether they still abide me, if in fact
    They ever did.
And when there's no answer, there's no hope

Of decoding the tones: seven local,
    Eleven long distance.
Then it's all I can do to reach out and touch

Myself. Last night I dreamt of a girl I dreamt
    I loved, and of the cop
Who busted me in Oxford, Mississippi,

And of my father who lost his life twice,
    Once in himself and once in me.
Outside, it's the world. Outside, it's the world.

I used to think I wanted my life back,
    But this *is* my life,
Gold moments between too much and not enough.

When something's too beautiful to simply
    Let go of,
You have to throw it away.

The Policy

Now that my death is bought and paid for
In San Rafael, California,
1650 Los Gamos Drive,

I can breathe a little, and I can sleep.
I have two years to wait,
Two years to choose,

Two years in the hands of the world
Before my life comes back
Into my own hands.

Two summers. Two Junes and Julys
With their bodies of water,
Bodies of women.

Two winters, too, where my father
Sold death among the walls
Of Minneapolis

Which he called hell frozen over.
But for now, summer comes on,
And dusk comes on,

And the air conditioner comes on
Wheezing its one song,
Hold on, hold on,

And the neon comes on across the street:
Acura, Mercedes-Benz,
Chicago Bar.

And tonight, in the blue dark of Kentucky,
My father could sleep a little
If he could sleep—

Now that I have bet my body that is the
One thing I have to his name
Against a fortune.

Style

I

You dreamed, continually, of water,
Of gulfs spreading out in darkness, of rain
Overflowing potted plants, a river
That for reasons you couldn't quite explain
Had childhood as its source and emptied, too,
Into childhood. In the background: "Misty,"
Muddled voices, a seascape—blue on blue.
You half liked it there, but woke up thirsty,
Stunned by the loud yellow alarm of noon.
The sunlight blasting through the trellised creeper
Made shadows on the bare walls of your room
That were as real as vine, only darker,
As you lay wondering who would find you
With blood blooming on the wall behind you.

II

I was surprised to find how light I felt
With most of the back of my head missing.
I recall, when I was twelve, French kissing
A girl named Star in the dark of a half-built
Duplex at the edge of our subdivision.
It was twilight. I hear my mother's voice,
My name. Women loved me like licorice.
It took me years to find a decision
I could make; now I want to change my mind.
I want to stand up and say "It's all right"
To the mirror. I want to fall crying
Into my father's arms, ask what happened.
At least I looked good, walking down the street
With all the well-dressed dead, the chic dying.

Four

One of the Forty-Eight

I was twenty, she was twenty-five,
    Our bodies perfect partners
For that most private, most intricate
    Of dances: above her,
Behind her, under her, beside her—
    It was love, and a love
That paid its dues in sweat, in the sweet
    Lingering bruises of love.

Afterwards, I'd get up to douse
    My head under the cold
Kitchen faucet and bring us back four beers
    (The first two we drained in gulps.)
Then I'd clench two cigarettes between my teeth,
    Light them, hand one to her,
And lie back and be utterly content to stare
    At my ceiling's sagging plaster.

While she talked of this or that in her crisp
    Northern voice so new to me,
Or did exercises in which she'd stretch each long tan leg
    Like an artillery gun aimed at some star,
Or wrote her name or drew horses on the legal pad
    I'd begun keeping by the bed
In the hope that sooner or later inspiration would come
    From this athletic muse of mine.

The list was my suggestion—that fateful list
    Of all those we'd slept with.
We made a bet on whose list would be
    The longer. I wrote down
My half-dozen or so conquests, and handed

The legal pad to her.
She paused, as though redecorating some room in her mind,
    And then she began to write.

And kept writing. Kept writing.
    And then it was a column.
And then it was two columns. And then she flipped over
    Onto the next page. "My lord,"
I couldn't help saying when she'd finished. "How many?"
    "Forty-seven," she replied.
"My god," I said, examining the list. "There are
    Four different guys named Joe!"

"Five," she corrected me, writing *Joe* again.
    "I'd forgotten you."
But just then—she must have seen I was hurt—
    She gave me a look and a touch
That said none of it mattered. And there was only
    That room, and *that* summer,
And I was happy again: to be her true love,
    To be one of the forty-eight.

Summer

How could we think that it would never end?
While each day was a little eternity,
We must have known the leaves were getting ready
To turn and fall—then loneliness again,
The chill, exquisite longings of autumn.
You woke to find it had become September;
I woke a little later to find you gone.
And suddenly what I would remember
Was wholly formed, irrecoverable:
The hundred-degree heat and the trouble
We had trying to keep cool in our shorts
Till the sun went down—me on the back porch,
Sipping Scotch and listening to Sinatra;
You in the bedroom, reading the *Kama Sutra*.

Tropical Inland Motel

No sea here—just a faint smell of the sea.
Open the window: the deep sky blues are
Giving over to the blues from a bar
Just down the street. Twilight begins softly;
Softly the streetlamps murmur on, amber,
As the token palm tree in the parking lot
Rasps in the breeze. Let's just stay in. We've got
A bottle and so much not to remember
Tomorrow! . . . acts, words, the name of this town.
As decadent as us in their back yards,
The dozing natives miss the evening news
They know by heart by now: sun going down
On all of the palm-ordered boulevards
And all of the flamingoed avenues.

Tropical Heat

He leans back on the mattress, nude, his head
Against the bare white wall because the woman's
Got both pillows tucked beneath her loins.
They're too hot and too tired to leave the bed.
He smokes and sips a beer, pausing to rub
Her raised bottom, the tan backs of her thighs.
She moans once, but doesn't open her eyes.
He thinks they could dump ice cubes in the tub—
Anything that might help to break this balm,
These sounds that, by this time, they hardly know
They hear: their breath; the endless monotone
Of the Casablanca fan; the radio
With its slow, sultry tenor saxophone;
The hot wind rustling through the royal palm
Outside the second-story bedroom window.

To a Woman Passing By

Say it was just a moment in a life
In which there ought to be more such moments.
For all I know you were somebody's wife
Or lover, emerging from the entrance
Of the shop, face poised, hands gloved, hair blown,
Your sculpted legs swishing your pleated skirt
As you strode up to ask me for a smoke,
Vivid as a girl I might have loved now gone,
Eyes of autumn. I found one in my shirt
And lifted the match in lieu of a kiss
Above the checkered scarf around your throat:
You, a stranger, vanishing into a car—
Out of my life, back into yours. . . . Call this
The most chaste of love songs, a thank-you note
To you who don't even know who you are.

The Woman with the Dog

For a long time, I used to fall
In love with women from distances—
Across a street, across a bar,
Across a hundred feet or so
Of sparse late-winter grass in a park.
I remember a woman
At the City Zoo in Houston.
She wore pastels, and the children
Whose hands she held in her hands
Didn't seem so much obstacles
As weights to hold her in the world
Of possibility. And a girl
Who waited tables in Mobile,
Her voice arriving as if
Across water. And a woman
In a gray suit in Orlando.
And a coed reading a book,
Eating ice cream on the steps
Of an old building in Atlanta.
And what would happen then was silly,
If not wrong. I'd imagine
Us together—not just the sex
But afterwards, drinking and eating
In bed with the radio on,
Always in her apartment
That would be neat, stylish, not too
Expensive, and filled with small things
I'd love because she loved them.
And then pulling on light clothes
And walking out into the late
Afternoon, into the city,
Talking about tomorrow
Or next week, but never
Any beginning, any ending.
Maybe it was my youth I wanted

Back. Maybe my imagining
Seemed to slow my death, and hers.
But I remember the woman
With the dog at Mansfield Park
In Tucson, Arizona:
Sunday afternoon, early spring,
What the falling sun did to her hair,
How at ease she looked in her jeans,
Her striped jacket and tennis shoes.
I guess I must have looked too far
Into her face and seen how happy
She was, the pleasure she took
Watching the black dog lope from light
To shade and back again. I saw
That she expected nothing more.
And that was the end of something,
Or maybe the beginning.
I understood how real she was,
And I was, and the city was.
And that moment, and the distance
Between us. Now I expect less. Now
I watch the women and let them go.
Now I let them have their lives
That have nothing to do with mine.

The Artist's Model

The light the morning of Soyer's death was clear.
It sifted through the three tall dirty windows
Of his studio. But he wasn't there—
Wasn't there among the deep blue shadows

Representing desire on the canvas,
Nor in the wood-framed mirror in which he
Painted himself, in shadow, painting me.
Outside, the city oddly without menace,

Traffic gliding down Seventy-fourth Street.
I remembered taking my clothes off those chill
Mornings when I'd come dressed like a Russian doll.
And still on the easel, all of me but my feet:

All body, all flesh, all paint, all surface,
The white shirt draped over my right shoulder,
A face both mine and not mine—distant, older,
As if he had painted his soul on my face.

The Years

And yet we'd do it all over again—
The success, the excess, and how desire
Got all mixed up with money, sex, the moon,
Till our house lit up like a house on fire.
Maybe it's the intensity we miss,
Those sleek maneuverings at night, when style
Seemed an end in itself, and which it *was*,
As things turned out. Tonight, in the dead still
Of the night, I lift a glass of amber
To all that's left, which is less than nothing,
Which is to say all I can remember
Of that feeling, that memory of a feeling.
Strange to want back what we wanted back then.
We were as good as dead, or better than.

Adult Situations

These moves we make
To do and un-
Do each other
Must be lovely
From a distance.

Such a music,
Such a twilight,
A surfacing,
A sense of style.
No end to it.

The white hotels
We check into
Keep standing. They
Survive each blond
Who comes and goes.

Cities go on.
The lights go on
In cities. Cars
Go to the sea.
The sea goes on.

What's left of us
Lasts in what is
Least us: in cars,
In the twilight
Of white cities,

In our houses,
In our closets—
Clothes we put on
In the hope of
Taking them off.

UNCOLLECTED POEMS

In Spring

Your morning opens, perhaps,
with madrigals the new dead are imagined to sing, or
angel-flight of ancient birds, the soft
places under their wings
warm gray and beginning to fill
with light reflected by the frail, changing
surface of a river they float over
like flags—

Though you are only a girl,
eighteen and afraid, pulling
the cool cotton dress around your body
like the arms of a lover, letting
your lips travel the rim of a coffee cup
as if it were the flesh of a man, as if
it could give back something more
than exotic smell and its bitterness.

2

You do what you can
to be modern in a country
of fields stitched together
with barbed wire the hunters cut through
before it has a chance

to rust, fields
mapped off by gravel roads
that refuse to swerve,
that make paths for the sun to follow each day.
You do what you can.

But you are late
or early for stylishness,
and all the cities and affluence you will know
are delicate tendrils the white motion
of your slender hands
can raise from the thawed earth.

3

The sun goes still for a moment in the sky;
hills stand up on every horizon,
long grass tilting with wind
and the meanderings of small animals
you cannot see. A cloud
reshapes its own abstraction, its edges
bronzed, as the guttural voices
of pigs swell between the rotting slabs that pen them in,
absent of language.

Next fall,
when the air above your land has darkened and shows
the draw and release of human breath, men will come
to shoot the larger sows in the head
with high-powered rifles, disassemble
the steaming meat with shining knives,
and leave you to your freezer full of pain.

4

At dusk you walk
through woods on fire with sound
and a last red revolution of light
down to the creek
to watch the water clearing itself
of the skeletons of leaves.

When your bare feet
are gone in a dark, teeming finger of current,
the stars start to come on
in patterns you are left to decipher.

5

The night is a theater of shadow
the cracked white walls of your house shine into
like frenzied cells.
You reel in the lamplight,
with bourbon burning under your tongue.

As you undress, not believing
the glow of your nakedness in the mirror,
the sculpted forms
your face and body have taken on,

as the night finally makes its silent love to you.

Once In Autumn

I rose before any other man, dressed in the dark, sucked up a warm puddle of bourbon, pushed the front door open and heard it fall off its rusty hinges behind me.

I wandered free, unshaved, across fields fenced off like the tiles on a huge kitchen floor. Memories leaped through the moonlight, set the trees trembling.

The sky began to pale, and I was average again. When I got back to the house and saw the door collapsed like a drunk bellboy, I dropped to the wet ground and slept till noon.

Another Rainy Night

From the church that seems a long way off in that
moment just before sleep, a bell flies ten, maybe twelve times
down Old Benton Road. I wonder how the sound managed to
keep itself dry. And what if, in the morning, when the dog-
woods are shaking their leaves like a wet poodle, I find a pair of
great bronze wings broken on my doorstep? The road silent, the
church nowhere to be found.

Summer and Smoke

What one admires in his plays is the desire
Almost despair, blue light that shows the ghost
Already shuddering inside the flesh.

Now, when lovers fall back from each other
To smoke, their sweat seems holy to them somehow,
Seems the shuddering ghost in overflow.

But that marble angel, gray against gray sky:
Is she stone only, or stone made wholly ghost,
Impacted music the sculptor couldn't unscrape?

However it is with her, she doesn't seem
To mind the way she's caught here like an anchor,
Wings frozen in that poise preceding flight

—As if this summer air held some despair,
Some desire deep enough to sustain her.

Ode to the Backs of a Woman's Knees

In the season
of summer,
when she stands
on tiptoe
to reach something
desired
high on its shelf,
or leans
straight-legged
for a drink
of water—
these,
sweet moons,
are your grandest moments,
the quick and subtle
beauty of which
I shall not let go
unpraised.
How often I've
mourned you,
bent back
upon yourselves
in the service
of her incessant motion,
or worse,
hidden
under hems of skirts
and impenetrable denim
of jeans,
undulating
like two plump
angelic actresses
who don't know
the curtain
has fallen already.

But for now,
twin tan mounds
faintly ravined
with white,
I behold you:
smooth arcs
the dolphins make
far off shore
in the sunset,
humps of camels
on the desert horizon,
two spoonfuls
of brown sugar.
Let me not
be led astray
by commercial calf
or democratic thigh.
It's you
I fall down before
in worship,
queen's cheeks
my lips aspire
to kiss,
circles of gold
my tongue trembles
to shine,
sable hills
my mouth waters
to rain softly upon,
tenderest meat
these male teeth
are electric for!

Haiku

1. *Child Playing in the Snow*

> O red-cheeked & wrapped!
> In you I see my small self,
> White angel risen.

2. *The Winds of March*

> Careful there, young man,
> Lest that horse-strong kite you hold
> Haul you to heaven!

3. *Mother's Day*

> Here's a rose, old gal.
> Adorn yourself. A dozen
> Will adorn your grave!

4. *August*

> Poor children called back
> To school, it's not there that you'll
> Discover new worlds.

5. *Christmastime*

> Here is the sad truth:
> I left the party alone
> And drove home joyous!

Before the Squall Broke Over

They were eating oysters and making all the jokes
One makes about oysters. The marigolds in mild light
Trembled with a particular sadness, and across
The bay the houses and the bright swaying boats
Mocked themselves in the blue water.
                                        A lone gull
Rose and fell along the shore as though controlled
By a string.

                    *

                It was summer, but cooler. The women
Wore sweaters and cupped hot buttered rums between their
        hands
Like holy lamps; the men sipped dark beers, fondling
The oyster shells wondrously as a child might fondle a coin.

They spoke of college and the money they'd made.
This moment felt right and inevitable as the stories
In a fourth-grade history text. Their futures lay
Before them in panorama, vivid unsettled valleys.

                    *

After a while, one of the women—the most strikingly beautiful
Of them—composed her face just so, and the talk slacked off
Like a waterfall run dry. They stared at her as if anticipating
A casual game of charades. Slowly, the woman parted her soft
Full lips and extended her tongue,
                                a rare flower opening.
They all saw it, the pearl, the tiny precious sphere,
And each man there, doomed to a fantasy he couldn't buy out,
Imagined a formally-borne cushion of fine red satin,
Upon which was balanced a gift for a king.

*

        Later, when the squall
Broke over, they all joined hands and ran for shelter.

Bad Sonnets

1. Women's Bicycles

Evening arrives with its muted pastels,
The buildings glow like pumpkins, and the thin
Moonlight glints off a row of parked bicycles.
Twenty-two, and already I'm a dirty old man,

Slouching on the steps of this women's dorm, waiting
For a friend. And there, in the parking lot become
Water with dusk and distance, a warping
Of reflectors as she paddles softly home.

Is it wrong that I want to occupy
That barless space, that sweet and chasmic lull
Between the gyrations of her tan thighs?
It would break my poor male heart if she should fall.

I love the slender form of these machines
With their black leather seats rubbed to a shine!

2. The Starlessness of the Fortieth Year

Maybe it's OK after all if you
Never write the great novel or make love
To the tan, oiled movie star in Rio.

Stretched out under an ordinary mauve
Sky, you count the stars that couldn't care less
About you. Blinded by their own cold light,

They've wheeled these forty years above your loss
And are little consolation tonight.
Even grand failures were beyond your reach:

Those heartbreak letters written and burned,
That Jewish girl who rode your hand so deep
Into orgasm she could not return.

What night requires, the singing dawn gives back,
Trustworthy as your inevitable heart attack.

3. "B" Movie

It seemed to you your life took two giant
Steps backward for each little step forward.
Even waiting in grocery stores, some tent
Of memory collapsed upon the gourd
Of your bald head which you'd refused to cover,
And under it you'd thrash humiliated
As under sheets pretending your lover
Was anyone whom you were not disgusted
By.
    And later, in the stench of your room,
You named each insect and traced its journey
Across the ceiling, or watched the streetlamps bloom
Like rotten flowers in garbage cans—the city
Undulating like an orgasm in the dark,
The bodies lying beaten in the park.

Seascape: Destin, Florida

The sea lifts in small blue arcs,
as if full of dolphins
who will rock soundlessly
all night
in the moonlight far offshore.

A pink sky drags the darkness
westward over the Gulf.

Along the highway
to Panama City,
the lights have staggered on,
their color frail
as the idea an orange has
of itself
before starting to grow.

It is this way,
It is that way,
the sea says—
only song it can remember
in the dark.

Cleaved Spheres

"They say a redneck and a hippie
should never get married
but we did it anyway."
                    —country song lyrics

Whether to drink the coke or snort it . . .
Whether to walk across the grass or smoke it . . .
Such decisions can finally become too much.

It came down to who was "gonna split"
or "high-tail it outta here." Turns out
we both did, leaving our shack to fall apart.

I won't apologize. I mean, never having
seen a damn whale, how could I know
if I wanted to save one? Horses

were all we really had in common.
And love of open fires, maybe. But you
can take your mushrooms and put them

back in a damp, dark place. I'll chew
my tobacco till the cows come home,
and you get up the nerve to milk them.

You looked pretty good, though, when you'd take off
your Indian sweater, beads, holey jeans,
bandana you never let me blow my nose in.

Remember how I took my boots off just
for you? Sometime when you're deciding
which white wine to buy, glance at a six-pack

and think of me.

Not This Life

but that other life
we keep losing in this one,
like the important phone number
crumpled in some crevice
of a beautiful woman's
chaotic purse. Plato says
this world is but a veil
of the world, a cleverly
designed backdrop against which
Hamlet is perennially unable
to decide. Bolton says
our careenings are as those
of moths in an empty church
the stained-glass air is sky to.
(Other times, Bolton says otherwise.)
But suppose—just suppose—
that the woman we spoke of,
looking for cigarettes
at a party, in a fit of impatience
spills the contents of her purse
out onto the coffee table.
She sees the wrinkled pink page,
and the phone number scored
on it in some untraceable hand.
She knows the number was
important, but, tipsy,
can't think whose it is.
She goes into her hosts'
kitchen to dial the number,
which she's told has been
disconnected. She wads up
the pink page, tosses it
into a tumbler where it grows
forlorn and anonymous as the gin-

soaked olive beside it,
and goes back to the party,
beautiful. So must we
return to this life.

Rack!

"Eat pussy, son?" the fat owner of the pool hall says,
      and the young man to whom the question
is addressed looks thoughtful. He may have just
      graduated from or just dropped out of
college, and he's deciding how much he wants this job.
      So far he's survived the interview:
can shoot a five-in-the-corner, a three-in-the-side;
      knows the troubling details of snooker,
cribbage, Amos 'n Andy; understands how very lightly
      you must tap a blackjack across the back
of an unruly patron's head, so as to subdue but not
      kill him; doesn't mind scrubbing a toilet,
making a greasy sandwich and cleaning up what's left,
      tricking the last dime out of a schoolkid.

There are any number of ways to answer the question,
      "Do you eat pussy?" and the youth
is choosing among them, trying to calculate the leer
      on the fat man's face. He could say,
"I never lick nothing nobody's dick's been in,"
      or, "If I want fish I'll order it,"
or, "I never did try it on account of I was afraid
      I might end up liking it."
The fat man, impatient, grunting, crosses his arms
      like two felled trees crashing
into each other. A cop walks in, nods toward the false
      wall behind which the endless poker game
goes on, laughs, says, "Thursday," wags his finger,
      says "Thursday" again, and walks out.

And while the young man is in the process of deciding
      whether he eats pussy or not, already
he's imagining what it's going to be like to spend
      one third of every day in this place,
where life is random and aimless as the universe itself.

He'll have to watch the working men
losing what little money they have left over each week.
He'll have to watch the tired alcoholics
feeding infinite rolls of quarters into computerized games
designed to rob them. Have to watch
old men misplacing memory like coins through torn pockets.
Watch boys coming of mean, hopeless age.
Watch a beautiful sixteen-year-old pressing her drunken
face against a jukebox, dreaming.

"How about it, son, eat pussy?" the fat man says,
wanting to get on with it.
The youth sighs, gives a fake lopsided grin, and replies
ingeniously: "Well, if I'm thinking of swimming
in a river I don't know, I make sure it smells OK first,
nothing bad washed up on the banks,
and then I dive right the fuck in and swim like hell."
The fat man looks serious a second,
then smiles like a hammock he's lowering himself into.
"Son," he says, "you got a job."
Moments later, as the youth is trying his apron on,
a player shouts, "Rack!" He grabs
A triangle of wood and hurries toward the table, feeling
as if some fallen angel were calling his name.

A Couple of Suicide Cases

1

"What could have possessed him?" people later
    will say. "He had his whole life
ahead of him."—that *him* being Jimmy Barlow,
    eighteen, attendant
at the Texaco on Highway 68 in Draffenville,
    who, come to dusk, is going to
drive the ten miles to Kentucky Dam, park
    his beaten Datsun, stroll
out onto the high concrete platform, gaze awhile
    at the first stars, at the last light
leaving the river, then casually—as if it were
    the most natural thing
in the world—jump, like a baby into the basket
    of its mother's open arms.
And in that split second before gravity
    gets hold of him, before
the water like a supercooled unbreathable air
    rushes up to take him,
he, Jimmy Barlow, will feel entirely free
    for the first time in his life.

2

"Goddamnsonofabitchingcocksuckingmotherfuckingasslicking-
    bastards."
        That's what Pat said when he broke down
the door to the roof of Kincannon Hall at Ole Miss, breaking
        his hand in the process. He didn't care:
he was a drunk ex-boxer from New York City, and flunking out.
        We were all drunk, too, following him like
disciples over the pebbles-frozen-in-tar surface—to watch
        the sunrise, to keep him from jumping.

We sat down beside him on the ledge facing east, unsteady,
     dangling our legs over the seven-story drop.
After a while, the stars began to pale in a sky that seemed
     suddenly huge, and then the horizon
was flowing through and through itself, like a watercolor
     in progress. Houses, fields, woods
came forward in fog. The world's dew turned into our sweat.
     It was May 1980 in Oxford, Mississippi.
We were young, drunk, ready to take on the whole South.
     There was no telling what might happen.
"Goddamnsonofabitchingcocksuckingmotherfuckingasslicking-
     bastards,"
     Pat said to the campus policemen who soon arrived.

Young Hispanic Man Looking at a Sculpture

Under the skylight, in the white noise of the fountain,
he walks around & around it—
clockwise, counterclockwise, now & then
bending his head back to witness
the high place where the colossus abruptly stops.
It's only the air surrounding it
he understands, because each welded sheet of iron
seems the flank of some alien army,
& the flat blackness of the thing
eats light.
Outnumbered, towered over,
he can't turn his gaze away.
He's standing still now, hands
clasped behind his back, & the passerby
sees only two silent figures
in ancient confrontation,
each withholding its terrible secret.

The Light We Dance Through

This is the afterlife. Her gin-
tinged breath came like a cool
injection in my ear.
We were dancing after midnight in this place
called 32nd Avenue, dancing
over cigarette butts & against
bodies not our own & through a light
of such blue density
it almost wasn't light at all.
But outside, there were stars,
& though all around us the city was playing games
with its deranged souls,
we danced three times around the parking lot—
a waltz, for chrissake, a fucking
waltz. That
was 1981, & each year
there are fewer & fewer people I'll admit
as my acquaintances,
& fewer still I'll dance with,
& it's probably the case
that, on those all-too-rare occasions,
the light we dance through is the closest
we'll ever come to any sort of afterlife.

Departure

Because it was a weekend morning,
You lounged awhile in the dustlight
Of your small room on 14th Street,
In that house like an old movie set.

I think maybe you sipped cappuccino
And smoked one ginseng cigarette,
Watching the neon of the liquor store
Lose itself under increasing sun

And raising the window to let the reluctant
Spring breeze bother your camisole,
You danced a moment to no apparent
Music—that city already strange.

And already your dozen or so friends
Seemed strangers. In one cruel week
We'd turned away from you, as if
To lose you before you were gone.

Left utterly alone, there is nothing
The heart can invent to numb itself.
All around you on the hardwood floor,
Your old life darkened in cardboard boxes.

I think, now, of those twenty black hats,
Black haloes your face paled under;
Jewelry, photographs, a few precious books;
Little shoes in which to make your exit.

If love is an awkward, scriptless scene
To be played out between two people,
I cannot write it: I am a pattern
Of breath and sleep that city will outlive.

And if poetry is a bond between
Two hearts, it is a bond too frail:
That night words failed, I, too, was lost—
To whiskey, memory, a photograph.

East of that city, the green fields
Are winding away beneath your gaze,
And here, west of that city, there is
No water deep enough to let me forget.

If I could look forward, I could see us
In Houston, in Atlanta—that South
No train will take us to, that South
We lost ourselves in so long ago.

And those cities, so far removed
In distance and time—can our small stars
Survive those bright lights? Our language
Be heard above the din of the million?

Tonight, a hundred miles away,
Our city, made of circles and squares,
Must be much the same as it was:
The bars, the buildings, the streets empty of lovers.

It is a city we can never
Return to—a dream, a green light,
An unfound door closed upon the past.
Our words echo through it and fade.

A Sort of Praise

Some morning in my city, a woman
Sits putting make-up on, expecting
No one, separated by one white wall
From the landscape that needs her.

And I—risen from fear, letting
My loneliness dissolve into the sunlit
Bough of a pine—will step out
And enter the shadows of tall buildings:

The sky glazed blue & gold, the streets
Drawing me to her door, the places
My feet hit like stones sticking up
Through the surface of some wide river.

And when our eyes meet, it will be
In the hue that happens when light finds dark,
In the secret music of worlds spinning true,
That we will move toward a sort of praise.

Summer's Lament

Now summer's gone, those long days of summer.
The light's still warm, but there's nobody down by the river.
Is this all there is? There has to be more.

Bronzing our bodies like gods beside the water,
We watched the blue-green world through Wayfarers.
Everything happened that's supposed to happen in summer.

A last dark chord dies in my dark guitar,
But I can't let go of what's already over.
Is this all there is? There has to be more.

Remember how we'd drive down by the river,
Risking the bodies we loved into the water?
And our luck held. Our luck held all summer.

We could not drown. We couldn't push the fever
Far enough; it rose, but broke in the water.
Is this all there is? There has to be more.

In the sky's white text, I read the cities of winter:
A world we did not ask for, and a future.
Now this page is all that's left of summer.
Is this all there is? There has to be more.

Childhood

My father holds the twenty-five to his head
      Like a seashell,
Like a transistor radio tuned to a channel
      Nobody else can hear.
He comes bounding down the stairs, almost like a boy
      On Christmas morning
Were it not for the fact that he's weeping
      And saying over and over:

"Do you want me to blow my fucking head off?
      Is that what you want?"
My mother doesn't say yes but doesn't say no.
      She's shaking,
Making a sound not with her mouth but with
      Her whole body,
A chanted, high-pitched wail that contains
      The chaos of the universe,

The rage that *is,* before language was.
      She clenches a clump
Of her hair in each fist, her hair
      Not the color
Of the sun going down so early in the day,
      But the color
Of a child's first clumsy rendering of that sky
      In fingerpaint—

The frail page he brought home, clutched to his chest
      Under a heavy coat,
And which he stood on the cold porch to admire a moment
      Before it ceased to matter.

Twilight

Somewhere, at the edge of a field
Dusk has set on fire, a horse
Lifts its broad head from the grass
And, like some beautiful machine,
Makes its way toward the sound
Of a bell in the distance.

Down by the creek, in the half-dark
Of honeysuckle and hickory,
The air itself is water,
While in the infinite expanse
Of failing sky, the evening star
Flares, reflected in the water.

Now the scent of honeysuckle
Melds with the sound of water,
And the child playing alone there,
Lost deep in his own music,
Drowns or disappears—is gone,
Beyond the reach of the bell.

The Lights at Southmayd Park

They flutter on, globular
Among the silver wings
Of pigeons who have forgotten
Where home was.

Through some stunted water oaks, Houston
Shows its machinated face
To what blood's left in the sun.

Those Chicano boys
From over on the barrio
Know how to scale high barbed wire
And walk a two-inch rail
Across a bayou.
I'd never make it.

And may not make it still.
The liquor store down the street,
Run by a surly Vietnamese couple,
Has gotten knocked over twice
This month already. They may close.

I could still take the Metro downtown.
There's one last bus past dark.
I could walk around wishing I were anywhere,
Oh anywhere else in the world.
I could go over to Telephone Road,
Pretend I was in hell.

I am in hell.
And I can't even make it
Over the bayou to Southmayd Park.
It will be winter soon.

Now the year's last softball
Lifts into chromium dusk.
No. It is the moon.

Tropical Courtyard

It is a rage against geometry:
The spiked fans of the palmetto arcing
Like improvised brushstrokes in the light breeze;
Late shadowplay, somewhere a dog barking.

Against the height of new and old brick walls,
Confounding stone, transplanted pine and palm
Lift in imperfection, as heavy bells
That would force order fade into the calm

Of azure and a faint scent of musk.
(Is it eucalyptus or just the past?)
There's nothing in this warm, vegetal dusk
That is not beautiful or that will last.

Desert Deluge

No rain nor hint nor hope of rain
    For months on end,
Then suddenly Thunderstorm Bertha
    (Your coinage)
Hits the city like a mass murder
    In a fast-food restaurant,
Taking no prisoners but the traffic
    Rush hour holds in bondage.

You're wasting time watching twelve screens
    Of *Divorce Court* in Target
(Which you pronounce Frenchwise, *tar-jay*):
    Infidelity,
Impotence, threat of castration, etc.
    Walk outside
And the world's gone crazy, horrendous wind
    Blowing housewives around

Like witches borne on black umbrellas,
    Empty shopping carts
Crashing into parked cars at forty miles an hour
    Like a go-cart race for blind ghosts.
Distant mountains to the south have disappeared,
    Great ships
Lost in fog—landscape become the sea's floor,
    New Atlantis.

You wouldn't think the world could be the same again,
    But the next day
(Like the day after your death, you think)
    It's as if nothing happened.

Page

Here is the page, half darkness, half silence, hoping
To find at last the way to you I could not find.

It contains all my boredom, sickness, and desire,
Those things I said in drunkenness, in rage or love.

Like water, it holds its drowned who are without names.
Like time, it was just a way of passing the time.

It lied now and then—I confess—for your pleasure:
Some misguided aim of overcompensation

For what was not only enough but too much.
Reliance upon language was its undoing. . . .

But someday it will be all that is left of me.
Death bothers its margins like gulls along some shore.

Tucson, Arizona
March 20, 1990

Notes and Dedications

The title, *The Last Nostalgia,* is from Wallace Stevens.

Breckinridge County Suite: To Rebecca

Conceived as a novella in verse, the *Suite* was written in Houston, Texas, in late 1985 and early 1986. I would like to express warmest thanks to Moorman and Juanita Hendrick of Breckinridge County, Kentucky, my gracious hosts whose farm provided the landscape that is central to this work. Along with the story line, the narrator's dramatic relation to the heroine, and the formal variations among sections, my concern lay with the exploration of that landscape in memory.

—J.B.

The sequence owes a specific debt to E. L. Doctorow's *Lives of the Poets* (from which the final stanza of the tenth section is adapted).

Days of Summer Gone

Some of the poems are dedicated as follows:
    "The Distance": for Rebecca Hendrick.
    "One World": for Rebecca Hendrick.
    "A Hymn to the Body": for Tammy Bolton.
    "Autumn Fugue": for Amy Wallace.
    "Photograph: *Being Sad*": for Tonya Parsons.
    "The Changes": for Frank Steele.
    "The Green Diamonds of Summer": for my father.

A number of poems are adapted from these corresponding sections of César Vallejo's *Trilce,* most with considerable and intentional liberties:
    "Your Sex": XIII.
    "The Story": XXXIII.
    "In Search of the Other World": III.
    "In Atlanta Once": XI.

"Lament on New Year's Day": VII.
"Days of Summer Gone": XV.

The New Cities of the Tropics

"Diptych": c.f. Jiménez's "Smoke and Gold," translated by Clark Zlotchew and Dennis Maloney.

"Tropical Watercolor: Sarasota": after Vallejo, *Trilce*, LXVII.

"Tropical Lament": after Vallejo, *Trilce*, LXXVII.

"Florida Twilight, 1905": most of the lines are taken directly from the final pages of Henry James's *The American Scene*.

"Little Testament": title from Montale.

"Daisy Miller at the Colosseum": the first two lines are taken verbatim from the Henry James novel.

"Aphrodite Holding a Seashell": see photograph of sculpture from Ephesus in Carol P. Christ's *Laughter of Aphrodite*. In Bowling Green, Kentucky, in the early eighties, Amy Wallace executed her Desire series, which consists of oil-on-canvas renderings of shells.

"In Memory of the Boys of Dexter, Kentucky": they are Billy Houk (though the poem was written before his suicide), Joe Wayne Pritchett, and others whose names I either never knew or have forgotten.

Adult Situations

"Ballroom Dancing in the Barrio": MFA party, South Tucson, April 1989.

"South Boulevard": for Arthur Smith.

"Near": for Little Johnny Cosco.

"Soon": after Horace, Ode II.15.

"The New Gods": the final line is lifted from Godard's *Breathless*.

"West Kentucky Quintet," "Back Then": for Greg Duncan; "Hell and Back": to an ex-friend; "Hell": for Billy Houk.

"Tropical Inland Motel": for Beth Schwartz.

"Tropical Heat": c.f. the movie *Body Heat*.

"To a Woman Passing by": after Baudelaire, "À une passante."

"The Woman with the Dog": title from Chekhov.

"The Artist's Model": the first, second, and last sentences of the poem are taken directly from Harriet Shapiro's essay of the same title in *The*

Threepenny Review (Spring 1989). The painting described is Raphael Soyer's *Artist and Model* (1987).

"Adult Situations": the title is from David Sanborn.

Uncollected Poems

"Summer and Smoke": from the Tennessee Williams play.

"Departure": for Tonya Parsons.

"A Sort of Praise": for Tonya Parsons.

"Summer's Lament": after Arseniy Tarkovsky, "But There Must Be More," translated by Kitty Hunter-Blair.

"The Lights at Southmayd Park": for Michael Goody.

"Page": the date the poet assigned this poem, March 20, 1990, ten days before his suicide, may perhaps be understood to imply that it should be taken as the last finished poem, though in fact it had been written the previous spring. The last manuscript poem or draft for a poem, however, was found a day or two after the poet's death, written out on a crumpled sheet of paper. *[Ed.]*:

In the House of Death

> I felt what I felt
> Were parts of me
> Starting to fall apart.
>
> Outside, the bare tree
> Shivered, and the black birds
> Shivered in the bare tree.
>
> I was afraid to walk out
> And pick up the morning paper
> Till well into the night.
>
> I counted the cigarette butts
> And I counted the empty bottles
> And I counted the spaces they left.

Sometimes, after rain,
The sun flared briefly,
And the black birds slicked

Their hair back in the bare tree.
(They knew, as I did, that it
Was just a matter of time.)
And I was afraid to open up
The paper and read of a world
That had stopped having

Anything at all to do
With me, unless it be
News of my own death.

And I put the cigarette butts
Into the empty bottles,
And put the bottles into empty sacks,

And dreamt there wasn't space enough
In the world to hold them,
And dreamt they'd outlive me,

And I slept and slept and slept
And slept and slept some more,
Not afraid not to waken, but to wake.

About the Text

THESE ARE NOT the complete poems. The poet himself estimated that he must have written about 500 poems during the eighties, and I myself have seen between 250 and 300 of them. It was his custom to gather into folders recent poems he felt like saving, at least for awhile, and to send them off for safekeeping to a chosen friend or two, thus compiling small homemade volumes to which he gave such titles as "The Tower of Babel" and "The Flamingo Hours."* Finally, he appears to have gathered everything he felt like standing by—or, as it must seem now, wished to be remembered by—into the large manuscript he presented as his thesis at Arizona. This was "The Last Nostalgia." It included the one book published during his lifetime, *Breckinridge County Suite*, which had been handsomely printed by Harry Duncan at the Cummington Press in 1989, as well as *Days of Summer Gone* (Galileo Press, 1990), which was in production at the time of the poet's death and appeared a few months thereafter. Added to these were two unpublished but evidently well-considered manuscripts, "The New Cities of the Tropics" and "Adult Situations," which make up a substantial part of the present book. The final section, "Uncollected Poems," consists of poems mostly found in earlier manuscript folders but which Bolton did not, for whatever reason, choose to include in "The Last Nostalgia." I did not think they should be lost.

I cannot claim to have honored the poet's choices perfectly. I came to believe that to do so would result in such repetitions of theme as to diminish the force of the individual poems. I also judged that Bolton had been too hard on his early poems. Some of them had the special freshness one finds in the early work of many writers—things seen and said for the first time. Nor could anyone have been certain that, had he lived, the poet, who was continually changing his mind about which poems to keep and where to place them, would have stuck by just those choices represented in what was to prove his final manuscript.

What I did was make an early decision to reprint all the poems I could

---

* I am indebted to the poet's friend, Michael W. Cox, for providing me with the folders of poems Bolton had given into his care. From a letter to me from Cox, April 5, 1998: "And last he [Bolton] handed me the blue box of poems, and he told me . . . that if anything should ever happen to him . . . I should get these poems to Donald Justice. . . . You mean, I said, like if you have an accident on the way to Arizona or something? Could be, he said. You never know."

find that had been published, not only in the two books, but in literary magazines, to which Bolton was, from beginning to end, an indefatigable contributor. That was the first principle.

Thus the first three poems in the section called "Uncollected Poems" are the first three poems of his to be published in magazines of some national circulation. They are not of the quality of the rest of the collection, but the fact of early publication would seem to justify their inclusion, if only for the record. After that I chose what, after many readings, struck me as the best of the unpublished poems, those that would make the strongest case for Bolton as the significant, various, and eloquent poet I believe him to be.*

The only other consistent principle was to exclude all translations. Like many American poets of the period, Bolton did a good deal of translating, all, in his case, from the Spanish. The translations, while fine enough in themselves, do not seem to me to break new ground. Their importance in relation to Bolton's original work can more profitably be seen in the numerous poems of the type known as adaptations or imitations, which take off from some foreign poem. These are identified in the notes as being "after" So-and-So. In Bolton's work the Peruvian poet, César Vallejo, is the most frequent source, but occasional credit is given also to French and Latin sources, even to the prose of Henry James. Three or four of Bolton's versions stick rather close to the originals; most depart to a considerable degree, some drastically and quite inventively.

There were no problems in establishing the text, once the poems had been chosen. No drafts of poems turned up, no manuscript revisions or worksheets. This poet seems rarely to have revised much, if at all. As friends have testified, the poems came with remarkable ease and fluency, as if already composed in his mind.

---

*A number of the heretofore unpublished poems have appeared in various literary magazines during the past year.